KNOTTED & BEADED

macramé jewelry

KNOTTED & BEADED

macramé jewelry

Master the Skills Plus
30 Bracelets, Necklaces,
Earrings & More

Morena Pirri

STACKPOLE BOOKS

Guilford, Connecticut

Published by Stackpole Books

An imprint of The Rowman & Littlefield Publishing Group, Inc

4501 Forbes Blvd., Ste. 200

Lanham, MD 20706

www.stackpolebooks.com

Distributed by NATIONAL BOOK NETWORK

800-462-6420

British Library Cataloguing in Publication Information available

Library of Congress Cataloging-in-Publication Data available

Library of Congress Control Number: 2020947439

ISBN 978-0-8117-3952-8 (paper : alk. paper)

ISBN 978-0-8117-6951-8 (electronic)

First Edition

Text and step by step photography: **Morena Pirri**
Editor: **Julie Brooke**
Jacket design: **Sally Rinehart**
Design and layout: **Dave Jones**
Jewelry photography: **Francesco Piccolo**

Printed in China

Contents

First Steps in Macramé

The first macramé I ever saw was in the form of knotted fringes used to decorate towels. But, little by little, I discovered a varied craft that unites different cultures and traditions from all over the globe. I immersed myself in this new world and started an adventure that captured me completely and has lasted for fifteen years.

I enriched my knowledge of macramé techniques through practice and by learning from people—mainly from Latin America—who I met at international craft markets. This growth period allowed me to find my own style and select the right materials for my work.

Every single creation is born spontaneously. When I knot threads, I communicate my emotions externally in perfect balance and harmony, and my mind relaxes as the anxiety fades.

The beginning of macramé—the art of tying ropes and threads using decorative knots to create wall hangings and embellish clothing and accessories—is often attributed to Arab craftsmen working in the thirteenth century. In fact, the skill was probably practiced in Ancient China. However, it is likely Arab visitors to Europe introduced the techniques to sailors who combined the macramé knots with the ones they traditionally used.

By the fifteenth century, macramé was popular in Spain and France, reaching England in the sixteenth century, and Italy in the seventeenth century. By the nineteenth century it was popular in the United States. The craft was revived in the 1960s and 1970s and used to create dresses, accessories, and jewelry. It then fell out of favor until the early twenty-first century, when its exciting possibilities were rediscovered.

Choosing the Threads

You can use a variety of different threads for macramé, depending on the look you want and what the item will be used for. The materials used to make macramé threads are vegetable fibers such as cotton, linen, hemp, or silk; and synthetic materials including nylon and polyester; these are often waxed. Leather can also be used.

For the jewelry in this book I have used a fine, waxed thread which creates elegant and refined pieces that can be embellished with beads, crystals, and semiprecious stones. These threads are between 1mm and 0.5mm thick; pieces made using very fine threads are known as "micro macramé."

Waxed thread is ideal for making macramé jewelry as the knots will hold well and, when you have finished making the item, you can cut off the excess thread and use a pocket lighter to weld the threads to secure them in place.

You can use a natural thread such as cotton, linen, or wool, but you must finish these threads by sewing them to the back of the item to secure them. Pieces made with natural threads are very beautiful, especially when the fringes are left loose to create boho- or ethnic-style jewelry.

Setting Up Your Workspace

To make your own macramé jewelry you will need a flat cork or wood board large enough to hold the work and suitable to stick pins in.

Choose pins with colored glass heads as they are easy to see when knotting. Use them to hold the threads in position while you work. Position them close to your hands, moving them as your work grows. There is no "correct" place to use them; simply add them when it is helpful. The step-by-step photos in the book show you where I like to use them.

You will also need a tape measure and scissors for cutting the threads, and a sewing needle and pocket lighter to secure the thread ends.

Getting Started

Before starting one of the projects in the book practice the knots until you are confident tying them. The knots used in each project are listed at the beginning of each one, and shown in the text using abbreviations which are also listed at the beginning of the project. Each item of jewelry is also listed as being easy, moderate, or advanced so you can choose the skill level you are comfortable with.

To obtain the best results, it is important to keep the knot-holder thread firm and tight with one hand, while you make the knots with the other hand.

Where necessary, I explain which hand to hold the thread with, which to make the knots with, and the direction in which to tie the knot.

Once you have decided which piece you want to make, assemble the materials you need and cut the threads; normally I calculate the threads should be eight times longer than the finished item.

To start, fold all the threads in half. Unless otherwise stated in the instructions, join each thread to your work in the center of the length.

Knot School

Lark's Head Knot (LHK)

You can make this knot with the threads placed horizontally or vertically.

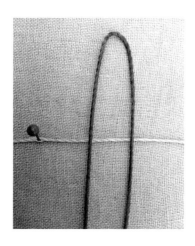
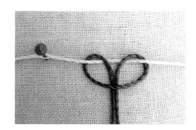
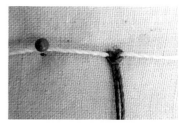

1 Place the light green (knot-holder) thread horizontally. Fold the dark green thread in half and place on top of the light green thread. You can use pins to anchor the light green thread.

2 Pass both ends of the dark green thread through the loop.

3 Tighten the knot by pulling the two ends of the threads down.

Reverse Lark's Head Knot (RLH)

You can make this knot with the threads placed horizontally or vertically.

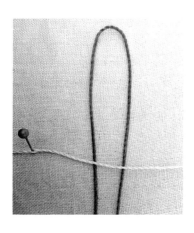
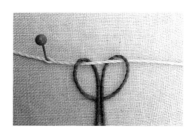
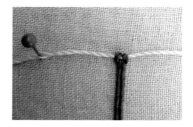

1 Place the light green (knot-holder) thread horizontally. Fold the dark green thread in half and place below. You can use pins to anchor the light green thread.

2 Pass both ends of the dark green thread through the loop.

3 Tighten the knot by pulling the two ends of the threads down.

Reverse Lark's Head Knot Plus Half Hitch Each Cord (RLH + HHEC) and Lark's Head Knot Plus Half Hitch Each Cord (LH + HHEC)

You can make the knot with the threads placed horizontally or vertically.

Reverse lark's head knot plus half hitch each cord

Place the light green (knot-holder) thread horizontally. With the dark green thread on the right-hand side, make a reverse half hitch knot (see above) around the light green thread. Repeat with the thread on the left-hand side.

Lark's head knot plus half hitch each cord

Place the light green (knot-holder) thread horizontally. With the dark green thread on the right-hand side, make a half hitch knot (see page above) around the light green thread. Repeat with the thread on the left-hand side.

Adding Threads to a Project

Sometimes you will need to add an additional thread as part of a project. You can use a square or lark's head knot—choose the one that best suits your needs.

Use a square knot to add a new thread in the place you need it.

You can add a new thread on a knot-holder thread with a lark's head knot, lark's head knot plus half hitch each cord, reverse lark's head knot, or reverse lark's head knot plus half hitch each cord.

Extending a Thread

If a thread has become too short to continue to use, you will need to join in another thread.

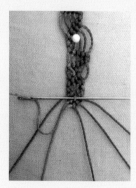

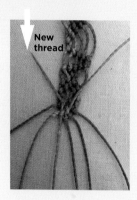

1 One of the threads in this project has become too short to use.

2 Use a sewing needle to secure the short thread at the back of the work.

3 Thread a new length of thread onto the needle and secure it at the back of the work. Then continue to tie the knots as described.

Finishing and Sealing the Thread Ends

Sewing and heating the ends of the threads will secure them to the back of the work.

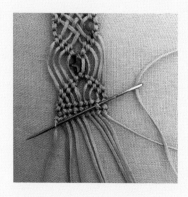

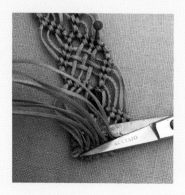

1 To secure the threads, use a sewing needle to stitch them to the back of the work, one at a time.

2 Cut the threads as close as possible to the stitching.

3 Use the flame from a lighter to gently heat the cut threads to melt them so that they attach to the back of the work.

Square Knot (SK)

You need four threads to make a square knot. Here two threads have been joined with a lark's head knot to make four threads.

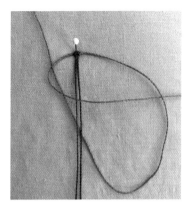 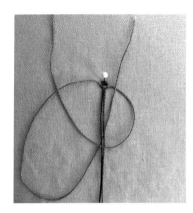 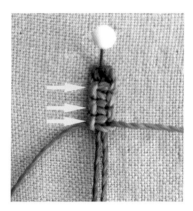

1 Place the light green (knot-holder) thread horizontally. With your right hand, take the first thread on the left-hand side (light green) and over and to the right of the other threads (dark green). With your right hand, take the first thread on the right-hand side (light green) and bring it over the light green thread on the left, under the dark green threads, and pass it inside the loop on the left. Tighten the two light green threads, keeping the dark green threads in position. This is a half square knot.

2 With your left hand, take the first thread on the right-hand side (light green) and bring it over and to the left of the dark green threads. With your left hand, take the first thread on the left-hand side (light green) and bring it over and to the right of the light green thread, under the dark green threads, and insert it into the loop made on the left-hand side. Tighten the two light green threads while, at the same time, keeping the two dark green threads still. This is a square knot.

When you are making a series of square knots, you can check the number you have made by counting the small knots indicated by the arrows. In this example, there are three square knots.

Square Knot Button (SKB)

This decorative loop is created using a series of square knots.

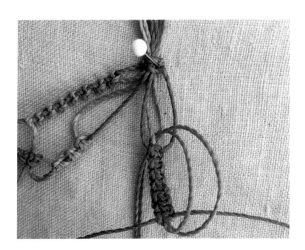 

1 Make at least seven square knots—more if you want a larger button. Take the ends of the two central threads (light green) and pass them through the threads above the first square knot (light green).

2 Secure the button by making a square knot with the dark green threads. To space the buttons out you can work some square knots between them.

Alternative Square Knot (ASK)

To make this knot you must use a square knot, so the number of threads required will always be in a multiple of four. The number of threads will also dictate the width of the work. For this example I used eight threads, and used them doubled, so that I had a total of sixteen threads.

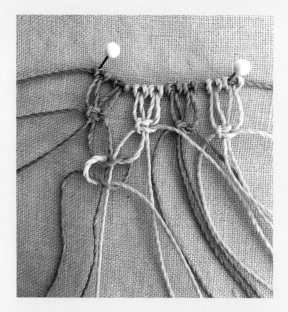

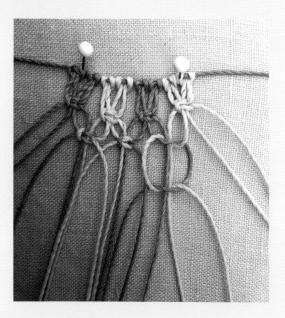

1 Make four square knots. Continue to make square knots but do not use the first two threads (in this example I have used two orange and two light green threads).

2 Complete the knot without using the last two light green threads.

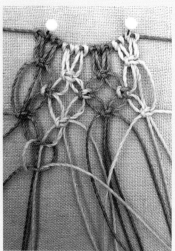

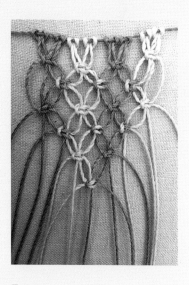

3 Make four square knots.

4 Make square knots, without using the first two orange threads, then use the next two orange and two pale green threads. Complete the knot without using the last two light green threads.

5 You can continue to repeat steps 1 to 4 until the work is the length you require. If you want, you can decrease the number of square knots as you come to the end of the work, as shown.

Half Knot Spiral (HKS)

You need four threads (two threads doubled and connected with a reverse lark's head knot) to make a half knot spiral.

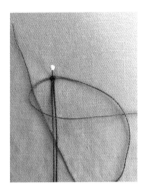

1 Place the light green thread horizontally. Bring first thread on left over dark green threads on right. Bring first thread on right (light green) over light green thread on left, under the dark green threads, and through the loop on the left. Tighten the light green threads. This is a half square knot.

2 Repeat step 1 until your have the desired number of knots. As you work, you will see that it automatically creates a spiral effect. It doesn't matter if you always do the same first part of the square knot or if you always do the second part. It is best to practice both ways.

Double Half Hitch Knot (DHH)

The double half hitch knot is made up of two repeated half hitch knots. It is very important to tighten the first knot. When making the second knot, take care not to overlap the first knot.

1 Place the light green thread horizontally. Using right hand, bring first thread from left to right over other threads. With left hand, loop dark green thread around light green thread and pass under light green and over dark green thread. Tighten. This is a half hitch knot.

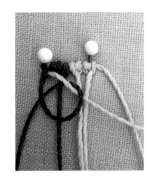

2 Keep the horizontal light green thread in your right hand. Hold the dark green thread in your left hand, make a loop around the light green thread, then pass the end over the dark green and under the light green threads. Repeat steps 1 to 2 with all the threads.

Making a Sliding Closure

Many of the necklaces and bracelets in this book use a sliding closure to allow you to adjust the length when you take them on and off. When sewing the thread ends to the knots do not stitch through the internal threads or the sliding closure will not work.

1 Position the threads from the necklace or bracelet so they face in opposite directions.

2 Position a 19 ⅝ in. (50cm) thread under the two threads and at a right-angle to them.

3 Use the new thread to make 5 square knots around the necklace or bracelet threads.

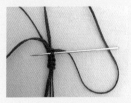

4 Use a needle to sew the thread ends to the knots to secure them.

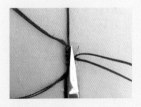

5 Cut the threads as close as possible to the knots.

6 Use the flame from a lighter to gently heat the thread ends to melt them to the knots.

Horizontal Double Half Hitch Knot (HDHH)

You can use any number of threads to make this knot.

Double Half Hitch Bar to the Right

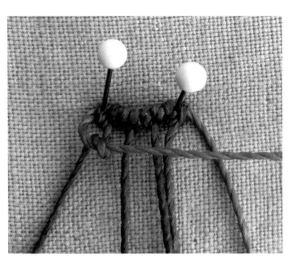

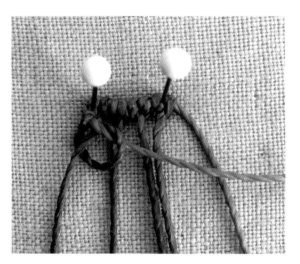

1 Place the light green (knot-holder) thread horizontally. Using your right hand, bring the first thread (light green) from the left-hand side horizontally to the right over the other cords. Using your left hand, loop the dark green thread around the light green thread from the front to the back.

2 Keeping the horizontal light green thread in your right hand, hold the dark green thread in your left hand and use it to make a loop around the light green thread from the front to the back. Tighten the knot. Repeat steps 1 and 2 with all the threads you are using.

Double Half Hitch Bar to the Left

1 Using your left hand, bring the first thread (light green) from the left-hand side horizontally to the left over the other cords. Using your right hand, loop the second light green thread around the first light green thread from the front to the back.

2 Keeping the horizontal light green thread in your left hand, hold the second light green thread in your right hand and use it to make a loop around the light green thread from the front to the back. Tighten the knot. Repeat steps 1 and 2 with all the threads you are using.

Diagonal Double Half Hitch Knot (DDHH)

Use the position of the knot-holder thread (shown in orange) to dictate the angle of the bar of diagonal double half hitch knots you want to make.

Diagonal Double Half Hitch Knot to the Right

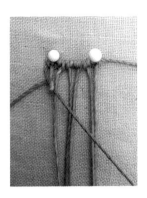 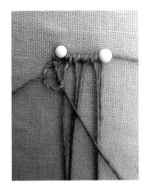  

1 Using your right hand, bring the first thread from the left-hand side (this is the knot-holder thread and is shown in orange) over the first blue thread and, using your left hand, loop the blue thread around the orange thread from front to back.

2 Continuing to hold the diagonal orange thread in your right hand, use your left hand to loop the blue thread around the orange thread from front to back. Tighten the knot and repeat steps 1 and 2 with all threads.

3 Using your right hand, bring the first thread from the left-hand side (this is the knot-holder thread) over the other threads. Take the second thread in your left hand and make a loop around it from front to back.

4 Continuing to hold the diagonal blue thread in your right hand, use your left hand to loop the blue thread around the second diagonal thread from front to back. Tighten the knot and repeat steps 3 and 4 with all threads.

Diagonal Double Half Hitch Knot to the Left

   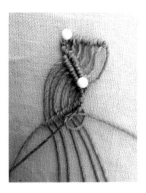

1 Using your left hand, bring the first thread from the right-hand side to the left over the other cords. Using your right hand, loop the second thread around the first thread from front to back.

2 Continuing to hold the horizontal thread in your left hand, use your right hand to loop the second thread around the first thread from front to back. Tighten the knot and repeat steps 1 and 2 with all threads.

3 Using your left hand, bring the first thread from the right-hand side toward the left over the other cords. Using your right hand loop the second thread around the first thread from front to back.

4 Continuing to hold the horizontal thread in your left hand, use your right hand to loop the second thread around the horizontal thread from front to back. Tighten the knot and repeat steps 3 to 4 with all threads.

Vertical Double Half Hitch Knot (VDHH)

Hold the light green (knot-holder) thread with a pin.

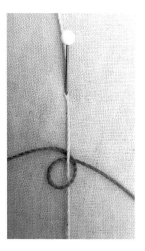

1 Pass the dark green thread from left to right under, above, and then again under the light green thread.

2 Bring the dark green thread from right to left by passing it over and then under the light green thread.

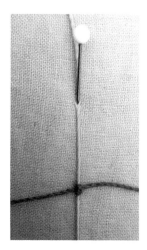

3 Tighten the knot.

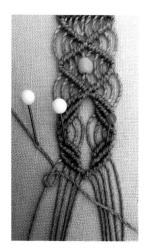

4 Add a thread with the vertical double half hitch knot. Secure the end of the orange thread with a pin and pass it first under and then over the gray thread from left to right.

5 Bring the orange thread from right to left by passing it over and then under the gray thread.

6 Pass the orange thread first under and then over the gray thread from left to right. Bring the orange thread from right to left by passing it over and then under the gray thread.

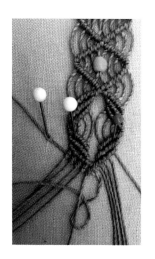

7 Continue to the third, fourth, and fifth threads. With your right hand hold the gray thread, with your left hand pass the orange thread first under and then over the gray thread from right to left.

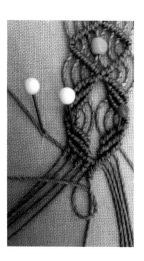

8 Bring the orange thread from right to left by passing it over and then under the gray thread.

Alternative Half Hitch Knot (AHH)

1 Using your left hand take the first thread on the left-hand side (shown in dark green in the photo). Use your right hand to loop the light green thread around it from front to back. This is a half hitch knot.

2 Holding the light green thread from the previous step in your right hand, use your left hand to loop the dark green thread around it from front to back. Repeat steps 1 and 2 until you have the desired length.

Inserting Beads

Beads add sparkle and visual interest to macramé jewelry. They are always added before the relevant knot is tied. Thread them onto the thread as you need them. If the end of the thread has become frayed you can wrap it in tape to help guide it through the bead.

Here are some ways in which beads can be added to a macramé design.

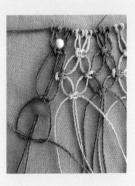   

1 The first green bead was inserted between the first and second square knots.

2 A second green bead was inserted onto the two central threads. Then beads were added before two bars of diagonal double half hitch knots were made.

3 Other green beads were inserted onto the second thread from the left-hand side and are framed by a diagonal bar.

4 This is the final design. You can also use smaller beads to create this style of design.

Reverse Double Half Hitch Knot (RDHH)

You can make this knot with the threads placed horizontally or vertically.

1 Using your right hand, take a thread on the right-hand side (shown in dark green) and, using your left hand, loop the light green thread around it from front to back.

2 Bring the light green thread under the dark green one and then back over it by passing it through the loop. Tighten the knot and repeat steps 1 and 2 until you have the desired length.

3 The photo shows three light green reverse double half hitch knots made with the left hand. Now use your right hand to make the knots with the dark green thread. Using your left hand, take the first thread on the left-hand side (shown in light green) and, using your right hand, loop the dark green thread around it from front to back.

4 Bring the dark green thread under the light green one and then back over it by passing it through the loop. Tighten the knot and repeat steps 3 and 4 until you have the desired length.

Accumulated Edge Using Double Half Hitches (AEDHH)

You can use an indefinite number of threads to make this design. The example shown here uses fourteen threads.

1 Using your left hand, take the first thread from the right-hand side and, using your right hand, make a diagonal double half hitch knot toward the left with the second thread.

2 Holding the first and second threads from the right-hand side in your left hand, and using your right hand, make a diagonal double half hitch knot toward the left with the third thread.

3 Holding first, second, and third threads from the right-hand side in your left hand, repeat step 2 with the fourth thread. Continue until all threads have been used.

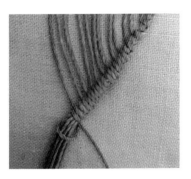

4 Holding all the threads except one from the right-hand side in your left hand, use your right hand to make a diagonal double half hitch knot toward the left with the single thread that is left.

5 Holding all the threads except one from the right-hand side in your left hand, use your right hand to make a diagonal double half hitch knot toward the left with the single separated thread.

6 Repeat step 5 until all the threads have been used.

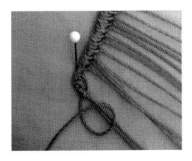

7 Using your right hand, take the first thread from the left-hand side and use your left hand to make a diagonal double half hitch knot toward the right with the second thread. Repeat using first, second, and third threads.

8 Holding the first, second, and third threads from the left-hand side together in your right hand, and using your left hand, make a diagonal double half hitch knot toward the right with the fourth thread.

9 Repeat step 8 until all the threads have been used.

Making a Zigzag

You can use any number of threads to create a zigzag using horizontal double half hitch knots. In the example, ten threads have been used.

1 Using your right hand, take the first thread from the left-hand side and make a horizontal double half hitch knot toward the right with every thread.

2 Using your right hand, take the first thread from the left-hand side and make a horizontal double half hitch knot toward the right with every thread.

3 Using your right hand, take the first thread from the left-hand side and make a horizontal double half hitch knot toward the right with every thread.

4 Using your right hand, take the first thread from the left-hand side and make a horizontal double half hitch knot toward the right with every thread.

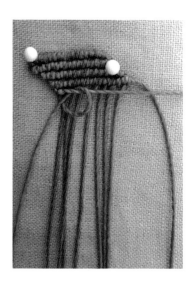

5 Using your right hand, take the first thread from the left-hand side and make a horizontal double half hitch knot toward the right with every thread.

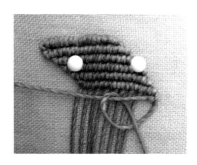

6 Using your left hand, take the first thread from the right-hand side and make a horizontal double half hitch knot toward the left with every thread. Repeat five times more.

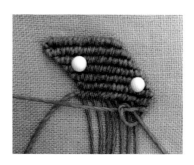

7 Using your right hand, take the first thread from the left-hand side and make a horizontal double half hitch knot toward the right with every thread. Repeat steps 1 to 6 until the desired length has been reached.

Making a Rhombus

This rhombus is made using diagonal double half hitch and square knots. In this example, the central section is always different, and so you can use it as the basis to make the one you prefer.

1 Using your left hand, take the fifth thread from the left-hand side and make a diagonal double half hitch knot toward the left with the fourth, third, second, and first threads.

2 Using your right hand, take the fifth thread from the right-hand side and make a diagonal double half hitch knot toward the right with the fourth, third, second, and first threads.

3 Make a square knot with the four central threads. Using your right hand, take the first thread from the left-hand side and make a diagonal double half hitch knot toward the right with the second, third, fourth, and fifth threads.

4 Using your right hand, take the first thread from the left-hand side and make a diagonal double half hitch knot toward the right with the second, third, fourth, and fifth threads.

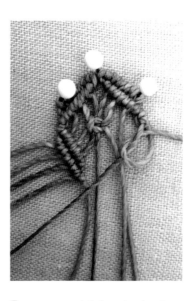

5 Using your left hand, take the first thread from the right-hand side and make a diagonal double half hitch knot toward the left with the second, third, fourth, and fifth threads. Repeat this step once more.

6 With your left hand, take the fifth thread from the right-hand side toward the left to make a double half hitch knot with the fifth thread from the left-hand side.

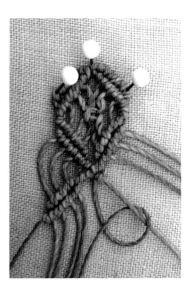

7 Using your right hand, take the fifth thread from the right-hand side and make a diagonal double half hitch knot toward the right with the fourth, third, second, and first threads.

8 Using your left hand, take the fifth thread from left-hand side and make a diagonal double half hitch knot toward the left with the fourth, third, second, and first threads. Repeat steps 7 and 8 on the other side, reversing shaping.

9 Take the two groups of three threads in the center and twist them together once.

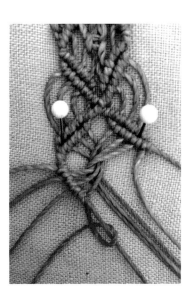

10 Using your right hand, take the first thread from the left-hand side and make a diagonal double half hitch knot toward the right with the second, third, fourth, and fifth threads. Make sure you use the threads in the right order.

11 Using your right hand, take the first thread from the left side and make a diagonal double half hitch knot toward the right with second, third, fourth, and fifth threads. Repeat this process on the right side using your left hand, the first thread from the right-hand side, and the second, third, fourth, and fifth threads.

12 Repeat steps 6 to 11, but change the center knot by threading a bead onto the two central threads. Then make an alternative half hitch knot with the other two threads on the right and left.

Projects

Crystal Cluster Choker

Clusters of sparkling crystal beads will catch the light when you wear this choker. The deep red thread used for the knots creates a dramatic backdrop for the facets of the beads. You can adapt the design to make a matching bracelet (see page 28).

You Will Need:

Four 98½ in. (250cm) lengths of ⅟₃₂ in. (1mm) bordeaux waxed thread

One 23⅝ in. (60cm) length of ⅟₃₂ in. (1mm) bordeaux waxed thread

One 11⅞ in. (30cm) length of ⅟₃₂ in. (1mm) bordeaux waxed thread

Fifty-two facted round crystal beads, ³⁄₁₆ in. (5mm) diameter

Types of Knot:

DDHH: Diagonal double half hitch

DHH: Double half hitch

RLH + HHEC: Reverse lark's head plus half hitch each cord

SK: Square knot

Abbreviations:

LH: Left hand

LS: Left-hand side

RH: Right hand

RS: Right-hand side

Difficulty Rating:

Easy

Size:

Knotted section 4⅜ in. (11cm), length of choker is adjustable

Starting the Choker

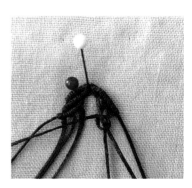

1 Position one 98½ in. (250cm) thread horizontally. Add three 98½ in. (250cm) threads in the center using a RLH + HHEC. Using your LH, take the 4th thread from LS and make DDHH to the left with the 3rd, 2nd, and 1st threads. Using your LH, take the 4th thread from LS and make DDHH to the left with the 3rd, 2nd, and 1st threads.

2 Using your RH, take the 4th thread from RS and make DDHH to the right with the 3rd, 2nd, and 1st threads. Using your RH, take the 4th thread from RS and make DDHH to the right with the 3rd, 2nd, and 1st threads.

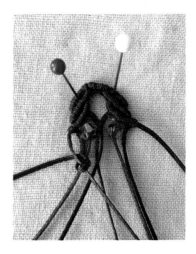

3 Thread 1 bead onto the 3rd thread from both sides. Wrap the 2 central threads around each other. Using your RH, take the 1st thread from LS and make DDHH to the right with the 2nd, 3rd, and 4th threads. Using your RH, take the 1st thread from LS and make DDHH to the right with the 2nd, 3rd, and 4th threads. Using your RH, take the 1st thread from LS and make DDHH to the right with the 2nd, 3rd, and 4th threads.

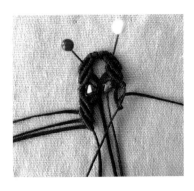

4 Using your LH, take the 1st thread from RS and make DDHH to the left with the 2nd, 3rd, and 4th threads. Repeat twice more.

5 Using your LH, take the 4th thread from RS to the left to make a DHH with the 4th thread from LS. Using your LH, take the 4th thread from LS to the left to make a DDHH with the 1st, 2nd, and 3rd threads. Using your LH, take the 4th thread from LS to the left to make a DDHH with the 3rd, 2nd, and 1st threads. Using your LH, take the 4th thread from LS to the left to make a DDHH with the 3rd, 2nd, and 1st threads.

6 Using your RH, take the 4th thread from RS to the right to make a DDHH with the 1st, 2nd, and 3rd threads. Using your RH, take the 4th thread from RS to the right to make a DDHH with the 3rd, 2nd, and 1st threads. Using your RH, take the 4th thread from RS to the right to make a DDHH with the 3rd, 2nd, and 1st threads.

7 Repeat steps 3 to 6 twice more. Repeat steps 3 and 4 once more. Using your LH, take the 4th thread from RS to the left to make a DHH with the 4th thread from LS.

8 Thread 2 beads onto the 1st thread, 3 beads onto the 2nd thread, and 4 beads onto the 3rd thread from both sides.

9 Using your LH, take the 4th thread from LS and make DDHH to the left with the 1st, 2nd, and 3rd threads. The 1st thread will be under the 2nd and 3rd threads, then the 2nd is under the 3rd thread, and finally tie the 3rd thread.

10 Using your RH, take the 4th thread from RS and make DDHH to the right with the 1st, 2nd, and 3rd threads. Using your LH, take the 4th thread from the left and make DDHH to the left with the 3rd, 2nd, and 1st threads two times.

Completing the Centerpiece

11 Using your RH, take the 4th thread from RS and make DDHH to the right with the 3rd, 2nd, and 1st threads. Using your RH, take the 4th thread from RS and make DDHH to the right with 3rd, 2nd, and 1st threads.

12 Using your RH, take the 1st thread from LS and make DDHH to the right with the 2nd, 3rd, and 4th threads. Using your RH, take the 1st thread from LS and make DDHH to the right with the 2nd, 3rd, and 4th threads. Using your RH, take the 1st thread from LS and make DDHH to the right with the 2nd, 3rd, and 4th threads. Repeat using your LH on RS, reversing shaping.

13 Using your LH, take the 4th thread from RS to the left to make a DHH with the 4th thread from LS.

14 Thread 4 beads onto the 1st thread, 3 beads onto the 2nd thread, and 2 beads onto the 3rd thread on both sides.

15 Using your LH, take the 4th thread from LS and make DDHH to the left with the 1st, 2nd, and 3rd threads. The 1st thread will be above the 2nd and 3rd; then the 2nd will be above the 3rd; and finally you will tie the 3rd one.

16 Using your LH, take the 4th thread from LS and make DDHH to the left with the 1st, 2nd, and 3rd threads. Repeat this step. Work steps 15 and 16 using RH on RS, reversing shaping.

17 Repeat steps 3 to 7.

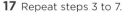

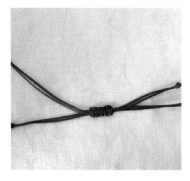

18 Add a 23⅝ in. (60cm) thread to the other end of the choker. Make a sliding closure (see page 12) using an 11⅞ in. (30cm) thread and 5 SK. Secure the ends on the back (see page 9).

Variation

Crystal Cluster Bracelet

Change the position of the clusters of crystals on the choker (see page 24) to create this pretty bracelet.

You Will Need:

Four 63 in. (160cm) lengths of $\frac{1}{32}$ in. (1mm) bordeaux waxed thread

Two $11\frac{7}{8}$ in. (30cm) lengths of $\frac{1}{32}$ in. (1mm) bordeaux waxed thread

Twenty-four $\frac{1}{4}$ in. (5mm) diameter faceted round crystals

Types of Knot:

DHH: Diagonal half hitch

RLH + HHEC: Reverse lark's head plus half hitch each cord

RLH: Reverse lark's head

SK: Square knot

Abbreviations:

LH: Left hand

LS: Left-hand side

RH: Right hand

RS: Right-hand side

Difficulty Rating:

Easy

Size:

Knotted section $2\frac{3}{8}$ in. (6cm), length of bracelet is adjustable

Making the Bracelet

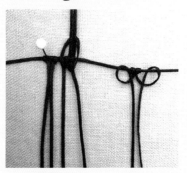

1 Position a 63 in. (160cm) length of thread horizontally. Add three 63 in. (160cm) threads in the center using RLH + HHEC. Add an $11\frac{7}{8}$ in. (30cm) thread with a RLH, to the opposite side as shown in the photo. (This will be used to make the sliding closure.) Work steps 1 to 6 of the Crystal Cluster Choker, then repeat steps 3 to 6.

2 Thread 1 crystal onto the 2nd thread, 3 crystals onto the 3rd thread, and 5 crystals onto the 4th thread, on both sides. Using your LH, take the 1st thread from RS and make DDHH toward the left with the 2nd, 3rd, and 4th threads. Using your LH, take the 1st thread from RS and make DDHH toward the left with the 2nd, 3rd, and 4th threads. Using your LH, take the 1st thread from RS and make DDHH toward the left with the 2nd, 3rd, and 4th threads. Repeat on LS, reversing shaping.

3 Repeat steps 5 and 6 for the Crystal Cluster Choker, then steps 3 to 6, then steps 3 and 4. With your LH, take the 4th thread from RS toward the left to make a DHH with the 4th thread from LS.

4 Sew all the threads to the back of the work, trim and seal (see page 9). Make a sliding closure (see page 12) using another $11\frac{7}{8}$ in. (30cm) thread and 5 SK. Secure the ends on the back, trim and seal them as before.

Blue Agate Cocktail Ring

A stunning blue agate bead forms the focus of this ring. The brown waxed thread creates a perfect setting, but you could use a gold-colored thread for a glitzy finish.

You Will Need:

Eight 19⅝ in. (50cm) lengths of 1/32 in. (1mm) Linhasita brown waxed thread

One 11⅞ in. (30cm) length of 1/32 in. (1mm) Linhasita brown waxed thread

One blue agate bead, 13/32 in. (10mm) in diameter

Four faceted round crystal beads, 3/16 in. (5mm) in diameter

Types of Knot:

DDHH: Diagonal double half hitch

DHH: Double half hitch

HDHH: Horizontal double half hitch

RLH + HHEC: Reverse lark's head plus half hitch each cord

SK: Square knot

VDHH: Vertical double half hitch

Abbreviations:

LH: Left hand

LS: Left-hand side

RH: Right hand

RS: Right-hand side

Difficulty Rating:

Medium

Size:

1 in. (2.5cm) in diameter, length of band is adjustable

Making the Setting

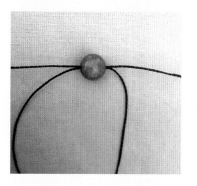

1 Thread one 19⅝ in. (50cm) thread through the agate bead. Thread one end of the thread through the bead from the opposite side to create a loop on one side of the bead and so that the bead is in the center of the thread.

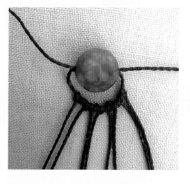

2 Add 4 threads into the loop using a RLH + HHEC for each one. This will be the RS.

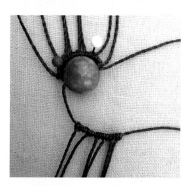

3 Add 3 threads using a RLH + HHEC on the LS thread as shown in the photo.

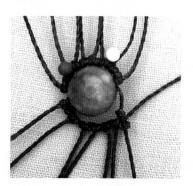

4 With your LH, take the first thread from the RS and make a DHH using your RH with the 7th thread from the LS.

 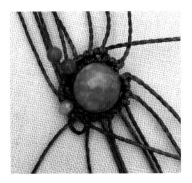 

5 Secure the 11⅞ in. (30cm) thread with a pin 4 in. (10cm) from the LS of the bead. Take this thread with your RH and using your LH make HDHH with the 2nd, 3rd, 4th, 5th, 6th, 7th, and 8th threads.

6 Thread a crystal bead onto the 11⅞ in. (30cm) thread, and continue to make HDHH with 8 threads.

7 Thread a crystal bead onto the 11⅞ in. (30cm) thread, and make a DHH with 1 thread.

Making the Band

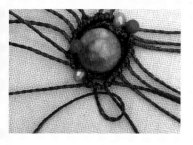

8 With your RH, take the 11⅞ in. (30cm) thread and make a DHH using your LH with the other end of the same thread. Sew the 2 threads to the back of the work, trim, and seal to secure them (see page 9).

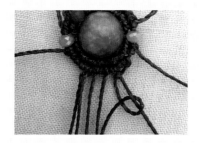

9 Don't work the 1st thread on both sides. With your RH, take the 1st of the remaining threads on the RS and make a VDHH toward the left with your LH with the 2nd, 3rd, 4th, 5th, and 6th threads.

10 Take the 1st thread on the LS with your LH and make a VDHH toward the right with your RH with the 2nd, 3rd, 4th, 5th, and 6th threads.

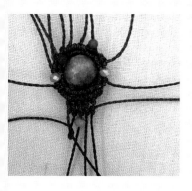

11 Thread a bead onto the 3rd thread. With your RH, take the first thread on the LS and make a DDHH toward the right using your LH with the 2nd thread.

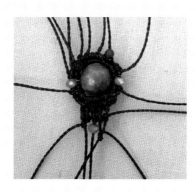

12 With your LH, take the 2nd thread on the RS and make a DDHH toward the left using your RH with the 3rd thread.

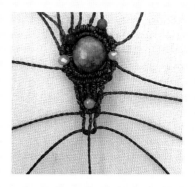

13 Use the 3 central threads to make a SK. With your RH, take the 1st thread on the LS and make a DDHH toward the right using your LH with the 2nd thread. With your LH, take the 2nd thread on the RS and make a DDHH toward the left using your RH with the 3rd thread. Repeat this step six more times. (To adjust the size of the ring, increase or decrease the number of repeats.)

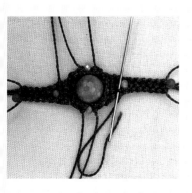

14 Sew the 5 threads to the back of the work, trim, and seal (see page 9).

15 Sew the 2 central threads on opposite sides of the back of the work, making sure the knots will not come undone. Finish the remaining 8 threads as before. Turn the ring right side out.

Zigzag Necklace

The center of this necklace features repeated angular motifs that are decorated with tubular beads which also feature on the ends of the thread fringe. A sliding closure means you can adjust the length of the necklace to suit the occasion.

You Will Need:

Seven 47¼ in. (120cm) lengths of ¹⁄₃₂ in. (1mm) Linhasita gray waxed thread

One 19⅝ in. (50cm) length of ¹⁄₃₂ in. (1mm) Linhasita gray waxed thread

One faceted round hematite bead, ½ in. (12mm) in diameter

Sixteen smooth hematite tube beads, ½ x ⁵⁄₃₂ in. (12 x 4mm)

Twenty-two smooth hematite tube beads, ³⁄₁₆ x ⁵⁄₃₂ in. (5 x 4mm)

Types of Knot:

AEDHH: Accumulated edge using double half hitches

DHH: Double half hitch

DDHH: Diagonal double half hitch

RDHH: Reverse double half hitch

RLH: Reverse lark's head

SK: Square knot

Abbreviations:

LH: Left hand

LS: Left-hand side

RH: Right hand

RS: Right-hand side

Difficulty Rating:

Medium

Size:

Knotted section 4⅜ in. (11cm), length of necklace is adjustable

Starting the Necklace

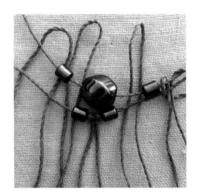

1 Thread a small bead, a large bead, and then a small bead onto a 47¼ in. (120cm) length of thread and lay it horizontally. Thread a small bead onto a 2nd 47¼ in. (120cm) thread, add a new 47¼ in. (120cm) thread with a RLH then add another small bead to the 2nd thread, and lay it below the 1st one horizontally. Add four 47¼ in. (120cm) threads behind the 2 horizontal threads as shown in the photo and secure each one with a RLH.

In the Know

Do not work the first horizontal thread because it will be used to create the neck tie.

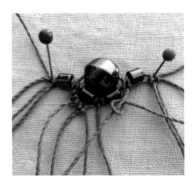

2 Using your LH, take the 4th thread from the RS and make DDHH to the left with the 5th and 6th threads. Repeat on the LS, reversing shaping.

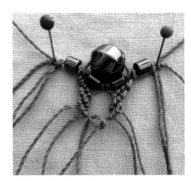

3 Using your LH, take the 4th thread from the RS and make a DDHH to the left with the 5th and 6th threads. Repeat on the left, reversing shaping. With your LH, take the 3rd thread on the right to the LS and make a DHH with the 3rd thread on the LS.

Design Variation

You can also thread the beads on alternate sides of the central motif, as shown here.

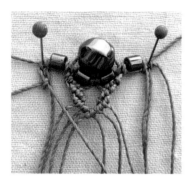

4 Using your RH, take the 1st thread from the LS and make DDHH to the right with the 2nd and 3rd threads. Repeat on the right, reversing shaping.

5 Repeat step 4 three times. Continue making DDHH with the 4th, 5th, and 6th threads. Repeat on the RS, reversing shaping.

6 Using your LH, take the 6th thread on the RS to the left and make a DDHH with the 6th thread on the left side.

7 With your LH, take the 1st thread on the RS and make a DDHH to the left with all 5 threads. Repeat on the left, reversing shaping.

8 With your LH, take the 6th thread on the right to the left to make a DHH with the 6th thread on the left.

9 Repeat steps 7 and 8.

10 Using your LH, take the 1st thread from the RS and make DDHH toward the left with 1 thread. Holding these 2 threads together in LH, make DDHH toward the left with 1 thread. Holding 3 threads together in your LH, make DDHH

toward the left with 1 thread. Continue until you are holding 5 threads together.

11 Repeat step 10 on the LS, making DDHH to the right, reversing shaping.

12 Holding all 5 threads from the left together in your LH, make DDHH toward the left using the 5 threads 1 at a time. Repeat on the RS, reversing shaping.

Completing the Centerpiece

13 Repeat step 12 on the RS, reversing shaping.

14 Thread a large tube bead onto the 6th thread from the left and a small bead onto the 4th thread from the left. Using your RH, take the 1st thread from

LHS and make DDHH to the right with the 2nd, 3rd, 4th, 5th, and 6th threads. With the 1st thread on LS, make a DHH around the 5 threads being held together. Repeat on the RS, reversing shaping. With the 1st thread on the left, make a DHH around

the 5 threads which are held together. Repeat on RS, reversing shaping. Hold the just-knotted threads in your left hand.

15 Using your RH, take the 1st thread on the right and make DDHH to the right with 4 threads.

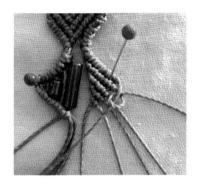

16 Using your RH, take the 6th thread from the RS and make DDHH toward the right with 3 threads.

17 Repeat step 16 with 2 threads and then with 1 thread. Using your LH, take the 1st thread from the RS and make DDHH toward the left with the 2nd, 3rd, 4th, 5th, and 6th thread. Remember to hold the just-knotted threads together.

18 With the 1st thread on the LS, make a DHH toward the left around the 5 threads being held together. Repeat on the RS, reversing shaping.

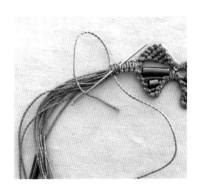

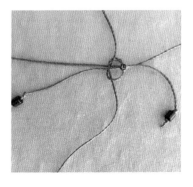

19 With your LH, take the central thread on the RS to the LS to make a DHH with the central thread on the left side. Repeat steps 11 to 19 three times, or more if you want a longer necklace.

20 Finish the knotting with 5 SK. Sew the 2 threads used to tie the 5 SK to the back of the work. Thread a long and then a short bead onto the remaining threads and tie a knot. Seal the ends (see page 9).

21 Position the ends of the unworked thread from step 1 so they point in opposite directions. Thread a short bead onto each end, tie a knot, and seal. Make a sliding closure using the 21½ in. (50cm) thread (see page 12).

Variation

Zigzag Earrings

The angular motifs and tubular beads that decorate the necklace on pages 32–35 can also be used to make these dramatic earrings, which have a shoulder-sweeping fringe.

You Will Need:

Ten 27½ in. (70cm) lengths of ¹⁄₃₂ in. (1mm) Linhasita gray waxed thread

Six smooth hematite tube beads, ½ x ⁵⁄₃₂ in. (12 x 4mm)

Six smooth hematite tube beads, ³⁄₁₆ x ⁵⁄₃₂ in. (5 x 4 mm)

Two silver earwires

Types of Knot:

AEDHH: Accumulated edge using double half hitches

DDHH: Diagonal double half hitch

RLH + HHEC: Reverse lark's head plus half hitch each cord

RLH: Reverse lark's head

SK: Square knot

Abbreviations:

LH: Left hand

LS: Left-hand side

RH: Right hand

RS: Right-hand side

Difficulty Rating:

Medium

Size:

2³⁄₈ in. (6cm) long (without fringe)

1 Lay 1 length of thread horizontally. Add 2 threads in the center using a RLH + HHEC in the center of each one. Thread an earwire in the center as shown in the photo. Add 2 threads in the center using a RLH + HHEC as before.

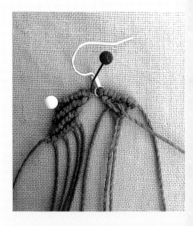

2 Using your RH, take the 5th thread from the RS and, using your LH, make a DDHH toward the right with all threads.

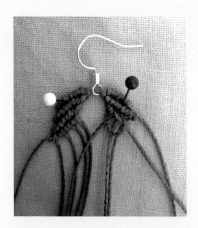

3 Repeat step 2 two more times. Then repeat steps 2 and 3 on the other side, reversing shaping.

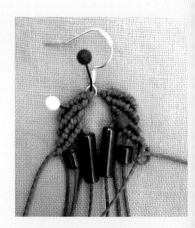

4 Thread on hematite beads as shown in the photo. Using your LH, take the 1st thread from the RS and, using your RH, make a DDHH toward the left with all 4 threads.

5 Using your LH, take the 1st thread from the RS and, using your RH, make a DDHH toward the left with all 4 threads.

6 Repeat step 5 twice more. Repeat steps 4 to 6 on the LS, reversing shaping. Using your LH, take the 5th thread from the RS and, using your RH, make a DDHH toward the left with the 5th thread from the LS.

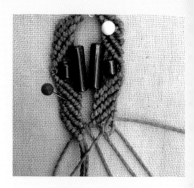

7 Using your LH, take the 1st thread from the RS and make DDHH toward the left with 1 thread.

8 Holding these 2 threads together in your LH, make DDHH toward the left with 1 thread.

9 Holding these 3 threads together in your LH, make DDHH toward the left with 1 thread.

10 Holding these 4 threads together in your LH, make DDHH toward the left with 1 thread. Repeat on the LS, , reversing shaping and working toward the RS.

11 Holding all 5 threads from the left together in your LH, make DDHH toward the left using the 5 threads 1 at a time. Repeat on the RS, reversing shaping.

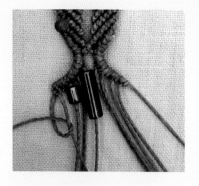

12 Thread the beads as shown in the photo. Using your RH, take the 1st thread from the LS and, using your LH, make a DDHH toward the right with the 2nd thread.

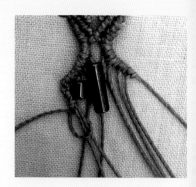

13 Holding these 2 threads together in your RH, make DDHH toward the right with the 3rd thread. Holding these 3 threads together in your RH, make DDHH toward the right with the 4th thread. Holding these 4 threads together in your RH, make DDHH toward the right with the 5th thread.

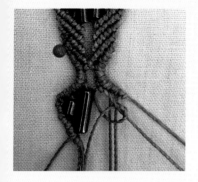

14 Using your RH, take the 5th thread from the RS and, using your LH, make a DDHH toward the right with 3 threads.

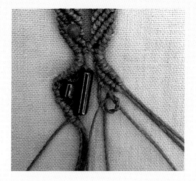

15 Using your RH, take the 5th thread from the RS and, using your LH, make a DDHH toward the right with 2 threads.

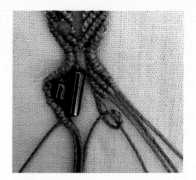

16 Using your RH, take the 5th thread from the RS and, using your LH, make a DDHH toward the right with 1 thread.

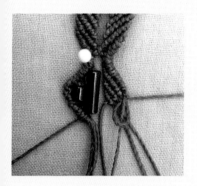

17 Using your LH, take the 1st thread from the RS and make DDHH toward the left with 1 thread.

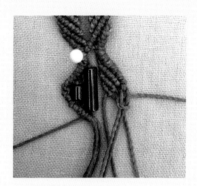

18 Holding these 2 threads together in your LH, make DDHH toward the left with 1 thread.

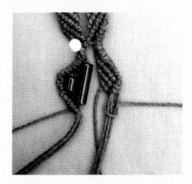

19 Holding these 3 threads together in your LH, make DDHH toward the left with 1 thread.

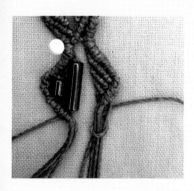

20 Holding these 4 threads together in your LH, make DDHH toward the left with 1 thread.

21 Make 4 SK with the external threads.

22 Knot each thread at the desired length and cut so they are the same length. Sew the two external threads to the back of the work and seal (see page 9). Make the second earring in the same way, following steps 11, 21 and 22 as written, and working steps 12 to 20 so that the earrings are symmetrical.

Oh-so-elegant Bracelet

Clusters of half hitch knots are framed by rose quartz and silver-colored beads on this elegant bracelet. The overall design is reminiscent of traditional wrought iron work.

You Will Need:

Three 39⅜ in. (1m) lengths of ¹⁄₃₂ in. (1mm) gray waxed thread

One 21⅝ in. (55cm) length of ¹⁄₃₂ in. (1mm) gray waxed thread

Six rose quartz smooth round beads, ¼ in. (6mm) in diameter

Twelve silver-colored round beads, ¹⁄₁₆ in. (2mm) in diameter

Types of Knot:

AHH: Alternative half hitch

DHH: Double half hitch

DDHH: Diagonal double half hitch

SK: Square knot

Abbreviations:

LH: Left hand

LS: Left-hand side

RH: Right hand

RS: Right-hand side

Difficulty Rating:

Easy

Size:

Knotted section 5⅛ in. (13cm) long, length of bracelet is adjustable

Starting the Bracelet

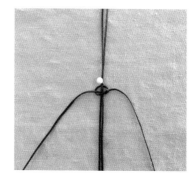

1 Take a 39⅜ in. (1m) length of thread, fold it in half, and position it vertically. Add another 39⅜ in. (1m) length of thread 4 in. (10 cm) below the folded end of the first length and secure with a SK.

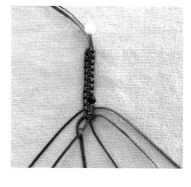

2 Make 9 SK, then add a 39⅜ in. (1m) length of thread with a SK. With your LH, take the 3rd thread on the LS toward the left and make DDHH with the 2nd and 1st threads.

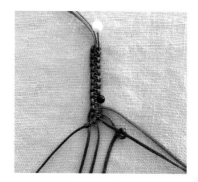

3 With your RH, take the 3rd thread on the RS toward the right and make DDHH with the 2nd and 1st threads.

4 Make a SK with the 4 central threads. With your RH, take the 1st thread on the LS toward the right to make a DHH with the 2nd thread.

5 Make another DHH with the 3rd thread. Repeat on the RS, reversing shaping.

6 Thread a silver bead onto the 2nd thread on both sides. With your LH, take the 3rd thread on the RS toward the left to make a DHH with the 3rd thread on the LS.

7 With your RH, take the 3rd thread on the RS toward the right to make a DDHH with the 2nd thread. Repeat on the LS, reversing shaping.

8 Thread a rose quartz bead onto the 2nd thread on both sides. With the central threads, make a DHH on the 2nd thread on both sides.

9 Thread a silver bead onto the 2nd thread on both sides. With your LH, take the 3rd thread on the RS toward the left to make a DHH with the 3rd thread on the left.

10 With your LH, take the 3rd thread on the LS toward the left to make a DDHH with the 2nd and 1st threads. Repeat on the RS, reversing shaping.

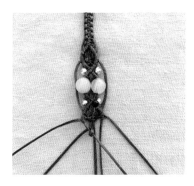

11 Make a SK with the 4 central threads. With your RH, take the 1st thread on the LS toward the right to make a DHH with the 2nd thread.

12 Make another DHH with the 3rd thread. Repeat on the RS, reversing shaping.

13 Thread a silver bead onto the 1st thread on both sides. With your RH, take the 1st thread on the LS toward the right to make a DHH with the 2nd thread. Repeat on the RS, reversing shaping.

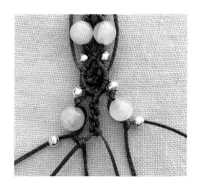

14 Thread a rose quartz bead onto the 1st thread on both sides. With your RH, take 1st thread on the LS toward the right to make a DHH with 2nd thread. Repeat on RS, reversing shaping. With the 2 central threads, make 3 AHH. There will be 6 knots in total.

15 Thread a silver bead onto the 1st thread on both sides. With your LH, take the 3rd thread on the LS toward the left to make a DDHH with the 2nd and 1st threads. Repeat on the RS, reversing shaping.

16 Make a SK with the 4 central threads. With your RH, take the 1st thread on the LS toward the right to make a DHH with the 2nd and 3rd threads. Repeat on the RS, reversing shaping.

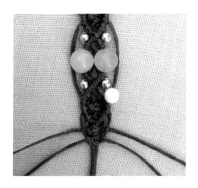

17 Thread a silver bead onto the 2nd thread on both sides. With your LH, take the 3rd thread on the RS and make a DHH with the 3rd thread on the left. Repeat steps 7 to 12. Make a DHH with the 3rd thread on both sides as before.

18 Make a SK around the 2 central threads with the 2nd and 5th threads. Make 9 SK around the 2 central threads with the external threads.

19 Sew the 2nd and 5th threads to the back of the work, trim the ends, then seal (see page 9). Make a sliding closure using the 21⅝ in. (50cm) thread (see page 12).

Rose Quartz Drop Earrings

A cluster of twisted threads in the center of the drops brings a lightness to these heavily knotted and beaded earrings. The design is enhanced by the inclusion of rose quartz and silver-colored beads.

You Will Need:

Fourteen 27½ in. (70cm) lengths of $\frac{1}{32}$ in. (1mm) Linhasita gray waxed thread

Ten smooth round rose quartz beads, $\frac{1}{4}$ in. (6mm) in diameter

Forty-six silver-colored round beads, $\frac{1}{16}$ in. (2mm) in diameter

Two silver earwires

Types of Knot:

AEDHH: Accumulated edge using double half hitch

DDHH: Diagonal double half hitch

RDHH: Reverse double half hitch

RLH + HHEC: Reverse lark's head plus half hitch each cord

RLH: Reverse lark's head

Abbreviations:

LH: Left hand

LS: Left-hand side

RH: Right hand

RS: Right-hand side

Difficulty Rating:

Medium

Size:

4 in. (10cm) long

Starting the Earrings

1 Position 1 length of thread horizontally. Add 1 thread in the center using a RLH. Thread a silver earwire in the center as shown in the photo. Add 1 thread in the center and on the other side of the earwire using a RLH.

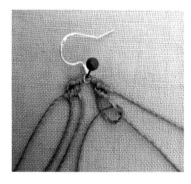

2 Using your LH, take the 3rd thread from the LS and, using your RH, make a DDHH to the left with the 2nd and 1st threads. Repeat on the RS, reversing shaping.

3 Thread 1 silver-colored bead onto the 3rd thread from the LS. Using your RH, take the 1st thread from the LS and, using your RH, make a DDHH to the right with the 2nd and 3rd threads. Repeat on the RS, reversing shaping.

4 Using your LH, take the 3rd thread from the RS and, using your RH, make a DDHH to the left with the 3rd thread from the LS.

5 Using your RH, take the 1st thread from the LS and, using your LH, make a DDHH to the right with the 2nd and 3rd threads.

6 Using your LH, take the 1st thread from the RS and, using your RH, make a DDHH to the left with the 2nd and 3rd threads.

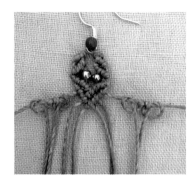

7 Add 1 thread on the 1st thread on both sides using a RLH + HHEC.

8 Using your RH, take the 3rd thread from the LS and, using your LH, make a DDHH to the right with the 4th and 5th threads. Repeat on the RS, reversing shaping.

9 Using your LH, take the 5th thread from the RS and, using your RH, make a DDHH to the left with the 5th thread from the LS.

10 Using your RH, take the 2nd thread from the LS and, using your LH, make a DDHH to the right with the 3rd, 4th, and 5th threads. Repeat on the RS, reversing shaping.

11 Using your LH, take the 5th thread from the RS and, using your RH, make a DDHH to the left with the 5th thread from the LS.

12 Using your RH, take the 1st thread from the LS and, using your LH, make a DDHH to the right with the 2nd thread.

13 Holding these 2 threads in your RH, make DDHH to the right with the 3rd thread.

14 Holding these 3 threads in your RH, make DDHH to the right with the 4th thread. Holding these 4 threads in your RH, make DDHH to the right with the 5th thread. Repeat steps 12 to 14 on the RS, reversing shaping.

15 Thread beads as shown in the photo. Add a new thread with a RLH in the group of 4 threads. Note that the LS is completed in the photo to illustrate this.

16 Holding all 4 threads from the RS in your RH, make DDHH to the right using 1 thread.

17 Holding all 3 threads from the RS in your RH, make DDHH to the right using 1 thread.

18 Holding 2 threads from the RS in your RH, make DDHH to the right using the thread with the beads.

19 Holding 1 thread from the RS in your RH, make DDHH to the right using the last thread.

20 Using your RH, take the 7th thread from the right side and, using your LH, make a DDHH to the right with 5 threads.

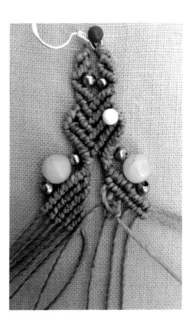

21 Using your RH, take the 7th thread from the RS and, using your LH, make a DDHH to the right with 4 threads. Using your RH, take the 7th thread from the RS and, using your LH, make a DDHH to the right with 3 threads. Using your RH, take the 7th thread from the RS and, using your LH, make a DDHH to the right with 2 threads. Using your RH, take the 7th thread from the RS and, using your LH, make a DDHH to the right with 1 thread. Repeat steps 15 to 21 on the LS, reversing shaping, as shown.

22 Thread beads as shown in the photo; only put 1 silver-colored bead in the 2 central threads. Using your RH, take the 2nd thread from the LS and, using your LH, make 2 RDHH to the left with the 1st thread.

23 Thread 1 silver-colored bead and make 2 RDHH to the left with the 1st thread. Thread 1 silver-colored bead and make 2 RDHH to the left with the 1st thread. Repeat on the RS, reversing shaping.

24 Using your LH, take the 7th thread from the LS and, using your RH, make a DDHH to the left with all 6 threads.

25 Using your RH, take the 7th thread from the RS and, using your LH, make a DDHH to the right with all 6 threads.

26 Using the 5 central threads on the RH and LH side, make a knot as shown in the photo.

27 Using your RH, take the 1st thread from the LS and, using your LH, make a DDHH to the right with each of 6 threads. Repeat on the RS, reversing shaping.

28 Using your LH, take the 7th thread from the RS and, using your RH, make a DDHH to the left with the 7th thread from the LS.

29 Put aside the 1st thread on both sides; they will be finished later. Using your LH, take the 2nd thread from the RS and, using your RH, make a DDHH to the left with all 5 threads.

30 Using your RH, take the 2nd thread from the LS and, using your LH, make a DDHH toward the right with all 6 threads.

Completing the Earrings

31 Put aside the 1st thread on both sides; they will be finished later. Using your RH, take the 2nd thread from the LS and, using your RH, make a DDHH to the right with all 4 threads.

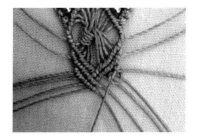

32 Using your LH, take the 2nd thread from the RS and, using your RH, make a DDHH to the left with all 5 threads.

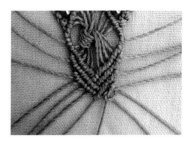

33 Put aside the 1st thread on both sides; they will be finished later. Using your LH, take the 2nd thread from the RS and, using your RH, make a DDHH to the left with all 3 threads.

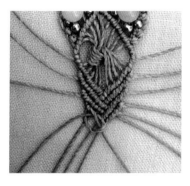

34 Using your RH, take the 2nd thread from the left side and, using your RH, make a DDHH to the right with all 4 threads.

35 Put aside the 1st thread on both sides; they will be finished later. Thread 1 silver-colored bead on the 2nd thread on both sides. Using your RH, take the thread with the bead from the LS and make a DDHH to the right with the 2nd and 3rd threads.

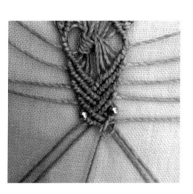

36 Using your LH, take the thread with the bead from the RS and make a DDHH to the left with the 2nd, 3rd, and 4th threads.

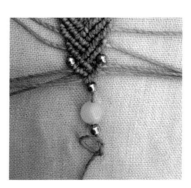

37 Thread beads on the 3rd thread from the RS as shown in the photo and tie a knot to secure them.

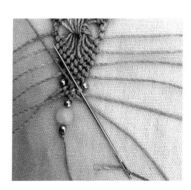

38 Finish the threads set aside in steps 29, 31, 33, and 35 by sewing them to the back and sealing the ends (see page 9). Make a second earring in the same way.

Star Earrings

Knotted strands of beige waxed thread using double half hitch and reverse lark's head knots are embellished with a scattering of star-shaped beads to make this eye-catching pair of earrings. You can also adapt the design to make a bracelet (see pages 53–54).

You Will Need:

Eight 29½ in. (75cm) lengths of $^1/_{32}$ in. (1mm) beige waxed thread

Twelve star-shaped hematite beads, $^5/_{16}$ in. (8mm) in diameter

Two copper earwires

Types of Knot:

DDHH: Diagonal double half hitch

RDHH: Reverse double half hitch

RLH + HHEC: Reverse lark's head plus half hitch each cord

SK: Square knot

Abbreviations:

LH: Left hand

LS: Left-hand side

RH: Right hand

RS: Right-hand side

Difficulty Rating:

Medium

Size:

2$^3/_8$ in. (6cm) long

Starting the Earrings

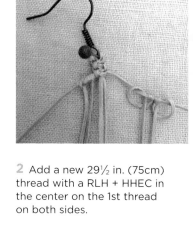

1 Thread a copper earwire onto a 29½ in. (75cm) length of thread. Add a new 29½ in. (75cm) thread with a SK and make 2 SK. The earwire should be in the center of both threads.

2 Add a new 29½ in. (75cm) thread with a RLH + HHEC in the center on the 1st thread on both sides.

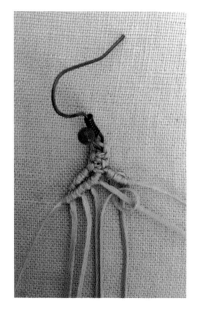

3 Using your LH, take the 4th thread from the RS and, using your RH, make a DDHH toward the left with the 4th, 3rd, 2nd, and 1st threads. Using your RH take the 4th thread from the RS and make a DDHH toward the right with th 4th, 3rd, 2nd, and 1st threads. Repeat on both sides, reversing shaping.

Completing the Earrings

4 Thread a bead onto 1 of the 2 central threads (it doesn't matter which one). Using your RH, take 1st thread from the LS and, using your LH, make a DDHH toward the right with the 2nd, 3rd, and 4th threads. Repeat using your LH on the RS, reversing shaping.

5 Using your LH, take the 1st thread from the RS and, using your RH, make a DDHH toward the left with the 2nd, 3rd, and 4th threads. Repeat using your RH on the LS. Repeat on both sides, reversing shaping.

6 With 2 threads on the LS make 10 RDHH. Repeat on the RS, reversing shaping.

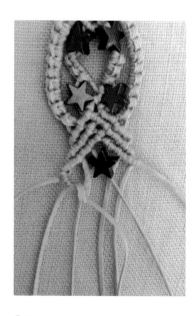

7 Thread a bead onto the 3rd thread from the LS and make 3 RDHH, thread 1 more bead. Repeat on the RS, reversing shaping.

8 With your RH, take the 4th thread on the LS toward the right to make a DHH with the 4th thread on the RS. Using your LH, take the 4th thread from the LS and, using your RH, make a DDHH toward the left with the 3rd, 2nd, and 1st threads. Repeat on the RS, reversing shaping.

9 Repeat steps 3 to 5. Sew the threads to the back to secure them. Trim and seal the ends (see page 9). Make a second earring in the same way.

Variation

Star Bracelet

This simple bracelet uses the same techniques as the earrings (see pages 50–52) to make a simple statement piece.

You Will Need:

Four 59 in. (150cm) lengths of 1mm beige waxed thread

Two 11⅞ in. (30cm) lengths of 1mm beige waxed thread

Six star-shaped hematite beads, ⁷⁄₁₆ in. (8mm) in diameter

Types of Knot:

DDHH: Diagonal double half hitch

DHH: Double half hitch

RDHH: Reverse double half hitch

RLH + HHEC: Reverse lark's head plus half hitch each cord

RLH: Reverse lark's head

SK: Square knot

Abbreviations:

LH: Left hand

LS: Left-hand side

RH: Right hand

RS: Right-hand side

Difficulty Rating:

Medium

Size:

Knotted section 5 in. (12.5cm) long, length of bracelet is adjustable

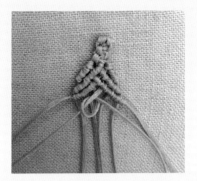

1 Take one 59 in. (150cm) length of thread and lay it horizontally. Add one 59 in. (150cm) thread in the center using a RLH, make 2 SK. Repeat steps 2 and 3 for making the earrings. Using your LH, take the 4th thread from the RS and, using your RH, make a

DDHH toward the left with the 4th, 3rd, 2nd, and 1st threads. Repeat using your RH on the LS, reversing shaping. Repeat on both sides.

2 Repeat step 4 from making the earrings.

3 Repeat step 4 from making the earrings on each side 4 times. With 2 threads on the LS, make 20 RDHH. Repeat on the RS, reversing shaping.

4 With the 3rd and 4th threads from the LS, make 4 RDHH. With the 3rd and 4th threads from the RS, make 4 RDHH. With the 2 central threads, make a DHH toward the left.

5 Thread a bead onto both central threads. With the 3rd and 4th threads from the LS, make 4 RDHH. With the 3rd and 4th threads from the RS, make 4 RDHH. Thread a bead onto both central threads. With 2 central threads, make a DHH toward the left.

6 With the 3rd and 4th threads from the LS, make 4 RDHH. Repeat on the RS, reversing shaping. With 2 central threads, make 1 DHH toward the left. Using LH, take the 4th thread from the LS and, using RH, make 1 DDHH toward the left with the 3rd, 2nd, and 1st threads. Repeat on the RS, reversing shaping.

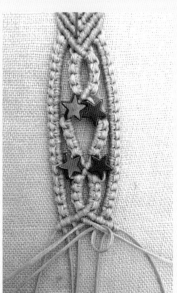

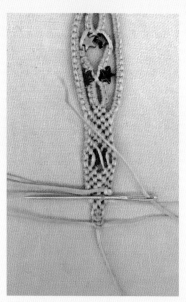

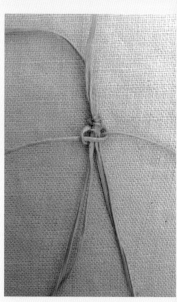

7 Using your RH, take the 4th thread from the LS and, using your LH, make 1 DDHH toward the right with the 1st, 2nd, 3rd, and 4th threads. Repeat using your RH on the LS, reversing shaping. Repeat another three times on the right and left. With the 4 central threads, make 2 SK.

8 Sew the threads to the back to secure them. Trim and seal the ends (see page 9).

9 Arrange the threads so they face in opposite directions and, with a new 11¾ in. (30cm) thread, make 5 SK to make a sliding closure (see page 12).

Starry Choker

A series of medallions filled with different patterns of interwoven threads make up this pretty choker. The half hitch and lark's head knots are embellished with star-shaped beads.

You Will Need:

Five 86⅝ in. (220cm) lengths of ¹⁄₃₂ in. (1mm) lilac waxed thread

One 21½ in. (55cm) length of ¹⁄₃₂ in. (1mm) lilac waxed thread

One 11⅞ in. (30cm) length of ¹⁄₃₂ in. (1mm) lilac waxed thread

Eight star-shaped hematite stars, ³⁄₁₆ in. (5mm) in diameter

Types of Knot:

DDHH: Diagonal double half hitch

HDHH: Horizontal double half hitch

RLH + HHEC: Reverse lark's head plus half hitch each cord

SK: Square knot

Abbreviations:

LH: Left hand

LS: Left-hand side

RH: Right hand

RS: Right-hand side

Difficulty Rating:

Easy

Size:

Knotted section 10⅝ in. (27cm) long, length of choker is adjustable

Starting the Choker

1 Position one 86⅝ in. (220cm) thread horizontally. Add four 86⅝ in. (220cm) threads using a RLH + HHEC.

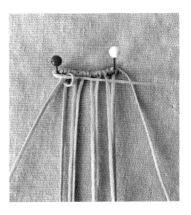

2 Using your RH, take the 1st thread from the left and make HDHH toward the right with each thread.

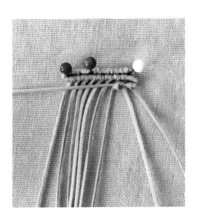

3 Using your LH, take the 1st thread from the RS and make HDHH toward the left with each thread.

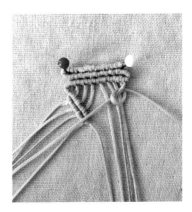

4 Using your LH, take the 1st thread from the RS and make DDHH toward the left with each thread. Repeat this process. Using your RH, take the 1st thread from the LS and make DDHH toward the right with each thread. Repeat this process.

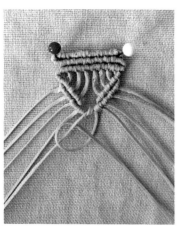

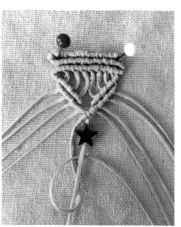

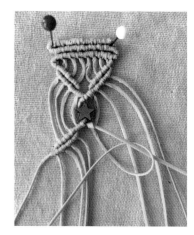

5 Using your LH, take the 5th thread from the RS and make 1 DDHH toward the left with the 5th thread from the LS.

6 Thread a bead on the 5th thread from the RS. Using your RH, take the 5th thread from the left and make DDHH toward the right around the thread with the bead.

7 Using your LH, take the 5th thread from the LS and make a DDHH toward the left with 4 threads. Using your LH, take the 5th thread from the LS and make a DDHH toward the left with 4 threads. Using your RH, take the 5th thread from the RS and make DDHH toward the right with 4 threads. Repeat this process.

Completing the Choker

8 Arrange the 3 central threads on both sides as shown in the photo, alternating 1 thread under and 1 thread over as if to weave them.

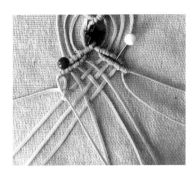

9 Using your RH, take the 1st thread from the LS and make DDHH toward the right with 4 threads. Repeat again. Repeat on the RS, reversing shaping. Repeat steps 6 and 7.

10 Make a SK using the 6 central threads, as shown in the photo. Repeat steps 4 and 5. Repeat steps 6 to 10 until you have 7 rhombuses. Repeat steps 6 and 7.

11 Using your RH, take the 1st thread from the LS and make HDHH toward the right with each thread.

12 Using your LH, take the 1st thread from the RS and make HDHH toward the LS with each thread.

13 Using your RH, take the 1st thread from the left and make HDHH toward the RS with each thread.

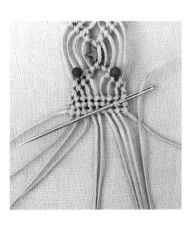

14 Sew 4 threads on both sides on the back of the work to secure them. Don't sew the two central threads.

15 Add the 21½ in. (55cm) thread to the other end of the necklace.

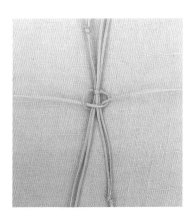

16 Make a sliding closure (see page 12) using the 11⅞ in. (30cm) thread and 5 SK. Secure the ends on the back, trim, and seal them (see page 9).

Beaded Openwork Choker

A symmetrical openwork design of interlocking circles creates a stunning focal point for this choker. It is decorated with silver- and jade-colored beads, which add extra visual interest to the design of lark's head and half hitch knots.

You Will Need:

Six 70⅞ in. (180cm) lengths of 1/32 in. (1mm) Linhasita green waxed thread

Two 27½ in. (70cm) lengths of 1/32 in. (1mm) Linhasita green waxed thread

One 21⅝ in. (55cm) length of 1/32 in. (1mm) Linhasita green waxed thread

One 11⅞ in. (30cm) length of 1/32 in. (1mm) Linhasita green waxed thread

One jade-colored bead, 13/32 in. (10mm) in diameter

Forty-two faceted round crystals, 3/16 in. (5mm) in diameter

Twenty round silver-colored beads, 1/16 in. (2mm) in diameter

Types of Knot:

AHH: Alternative half hitch

DDHH: Diagonal double half hitch

HDHH: Horizontal double half hitch

RDHH: Reverse double half hitch

RLH: Reverse lark's head

RLH + HH: Reverse lark's head plus half hitch

SK: Square knot

Abbreviations:

LH: Left hand

LS: Left-hand side

RH: Right hand

RS: Right-hand side

Difficulty Rating:

Advanced

Size:

Knotted section 6⅜ in. (16cm) long, length of choker is adjustable

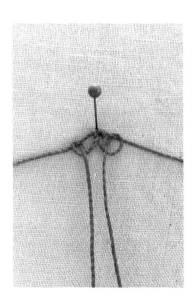

1 Position one 70⅞ in. (180cm) length of thread horizontally. Add a 2nd 70⅞ in. (180cm) length of thread in the center using a RLH + HH with each thread.

2 Using your RH, take the 1st thread from LS and make HDHH to the right with the 2nd, 3rd, and 4th threads. Using your LH, take the 1st thread from RS and make HDHH to the left with the 2nd, 3rd, and 4th threads. Using your RH, take the 1st thread from LS and make HDHH to the right with the 2nd and 3rd threads. Add a new 70⅞ in. (180cm) thread with a RLH, and make a DHH with the 4th thread.

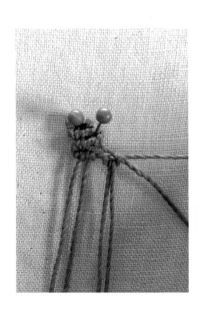

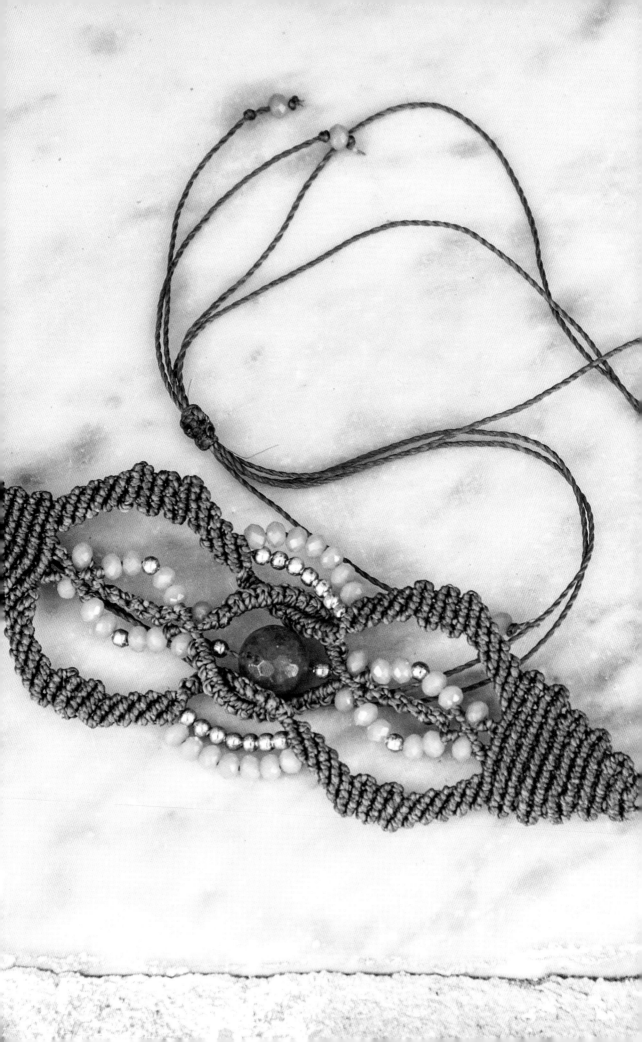

Making the Centerpiece

3 Using your LH, take the 1st thread from RS and make HDHH to the left with the 2nd, 3rd, 4th, 5th, and 6th threads. Using your RH, take the 1st thread from LS and make HDHH to the right with the 2nd thread. Add a 70⅞ in. (180cm) thread with a RLH and make DHH with the 3rd, 4th, 5th, and 6th threads.

4 Using your LH, take the 1st thread from RS and make HDHH to the left with 7 threads. Using your RH, take the 1st thread from LS and make HDHH to the right with the 2nd, 3rd, 4th, 5th, 6th, and 7th threads. Add a new 70⅞ in. (180cm) thread with a RLH, and make a DHH with the 8th thread. Using your LH, take the 1st thread from RS and make HDHH to the left with 10 threads. Using your RH, take the 1st thread from LS and make HDHH to the right with the 2nd thread. Add a 70⅞ in. (180cm)

thread with a RLH, and use to make a DHH with the 8 threads. Make another 4 HDHH bars with 12 threads. Using your LH, take the 4th thread from LS and make DDHH to the left with the 3rd, 2nd, and 1st threads.

5 Using your LH, take the 4th thread from LS and make DDHH to the left with the 3rd, 2nd, and 1st threads.

6 Make 3 more DDHH knot bars. Using your RH, take the 1st thread from LS and make HDHH to the right with the 2nd, 3rd, and 4th threads.

7 Make 3 more HDHH bars. Using your RH, take the 1st thread from LS and make 5 DDHH knot bars to the right with the 2nd, 3rd, and 4th threads.

8 Using your RH, take the 4th thread from RS and make DDHH to the right with the 3rd, 2nd, and 1st threads. Repeat steps 5 to 7 on the other side of the motif, reversing shaping.

9 Using your RH, take the 1st thread from LS of 4 central threads and make 1 DDHH knot to the right with 2nd thread.

10 Using your LH, take the 1st thread from RS of the 4 central threads and make 1 DDHH knot to the left with the 2nd thread.

11 Using your LH, take the 2nd thread from RS and make 1 DDHH to the left with the 2nd thread from LS.

12 Thread a crystal onto the exterior threads on both sides. Using your LH, take the 2nd thread from LS and make 1 DDHH to the left with the 1st thread. Repeat on RS, reversing shaping.

13 Thread 2 crystals, 1 silver bead, then 2 crystals on both sides. Make 4 AHH with the 2 central threads. Using your RH, take the 1st thread on LS and make 1 DDHH to the right with the 2nd thread.

14 Using your LH, take the 2nd thread from RS and make 1 DDHH to the left with the 2nd thread from LS.

15 Thread a crystal onto the exterior threads on both sides. Using your LH, take the 2nd thread from LS and make a DDHH to the left with the 1st thread. Repeat on RS, reversing shaping. On both sides, make 13 RDHH with the external thread around the inner threads.

16 With the 4th thread from LS, make 10 RDHH around the 3rd thread from LS. Repeat on RS, reversing shaping.

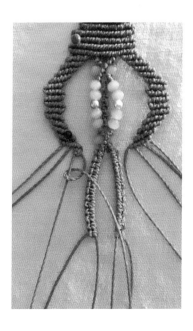

17 Thread 7 crystals and 7 silver beads onto both sides. Twist the knotted threads together as shown in the photo. Using your RH, take the 3rd thread from RS and make a DDHH to the right with the 2nd and 1st threads.

18 Using your RH, take the 4th thread from RS and make a DDHH to the right with the 3rd, 2nd, and 1st threads. Repeat on the LS, reversing shaping.

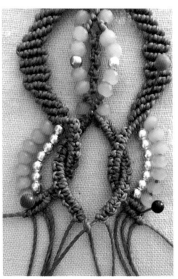

Completing the Choker

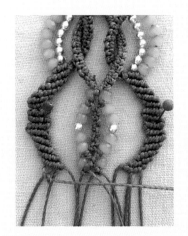

19 Using your LH, take the 2nd thread from RS of the 4 central threads and make 1 DDHH to the left with the 2nd thread from LS. Repeat steps 6 to 14 on both sides, reversing shaping. Thread a crystal onto the exterior threads on both sides. Using your LH, take the 2nd thread from LS and make a DDHH to the left with the 1st thread. Repeat on RS, reversing shaping.

20 Using your RH, take the 1st thread on LS and make 1 HDHH to the right with all threads. Make 3 more HDHH bars with all 12 threads. Make 9 HDHH bars, decreasing the number of threads at the same points where they were added in steps 2 to 4. Put the un-knotted threads to the back of the work and, when you have finished, sew them to the back, trim, and seal the ends (see page 9). You will have 2 unfinished threads. If they are not long enough to work with, add 1 that is 27½ in. (70cm) long. Add another 27½ in. (70cm) thread to the other end of the necklace and, with the 21½ in. (50cm) thread,

make a sliding closure (see page 12). Thread a crystal onto the end of each external thread and secure with a knot.

21 Thread 1 silver bead, 1 jade bead, and then 1 silver bead onto the 11⅛ in. (30cm) length of thread. Sew to the center-back of the necklace (see page 9).

Spiral Earrings

Rows of diagonal double half hitch knots and crystal beads are twisted as you work to make these eye-catching earrings and matching bracelet (see pages 67–69).

You Will Need:

Twelve 23⅝ in. (60cm) lengths of 1/64 in. (0.5mm) blue waxed thread

Two silver earwires

128 crystal beads 1/16 in. (2mm) in diameter

Types of Knot:

DDHH: Diagonal double half hitch

RLH + HHEC: Reverse lark's head plus half hitch each cord

Abbreviations:

LH: Left hand

LS: Left-hand side

RH: Right hand

RS: Right-hand side

Difficulty Rating:

Medium

Size:

2¾ in. (7cm) long

Starting the Earrings

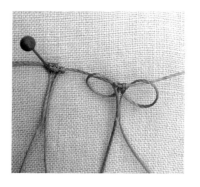

1 Position 1 thread horizontally. Add 5 threads in the center using a RLH + HHEC in the center of each one.

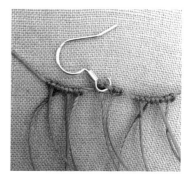

2 Thread a silver earwire in the center as shown in the photo.

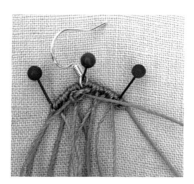

3 Using your LH, take the 6th thread from the RS and, using your RH, make a DDHH toward the left with all 6 threads. Using your RH, take the 6th thread from the RS and, using your LH, make a DDHH toward the right with all 5 threads.

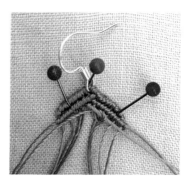

4 Using your RH, take the 6th thread from the LS and, using your LH, make a DDHH toward the right with all 6 threads. Using your LH, take the 6th thread from the LS and, using your RH, make a DDHH toward the left with all 5 threads.

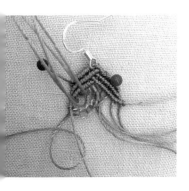

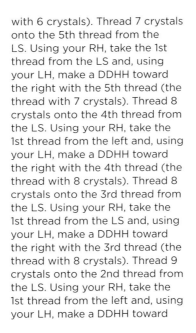

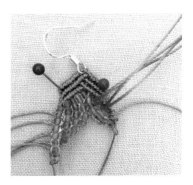

5 Thread 6 crystals onto the 6th thread from the LS. Taking care to use the thread with the beads first, arrange the other threads upward as shown in the photo. Using your RH, take the 1st thread from the LS and, using your LH, make a DDHH toward the right with the 6th thread (the thread

with 6 crystals). Thread 7 crystals onto the 5th thread from the LS. Using your RH, take the 1st thread from the LS and, using your LH, make a DDHH toward the right with the 5th thread (the thread with 7 crystals). Thread 8 crystals onto the 4th thread from the LS. Using your RH, take the 1st thread from the left and, using your LH, make a DDHH toward the right with the 4th thread (the thread with 8 crystals). Thread 8 crystals onto the 3rd thread from the LS. Using your RH, take the 1st thread from the LS and, using your LH, make a DDHH toward the right with the 3rd thread (the thread with 8 crystals). Thread 9 crystals onto the 2nd thread from the LS. Using your RH, take the 1st thread from the left and, using your LH, make a DDHH toward

the right with the 2nd thread (the thread with 9 crystals).

6 Repeat step 5 on the RS, reversing shaping.

7 Using your LH, take the 1st thread on the RS and, using your RH, make a DDHH toward the left with all 5 threads.

8 Repeat step 7 nine times more. Repeat steps 7 and 8 on the LS, reversing shaping.

9 Using your LH, take the 6th thread from the RS and, using your RH, make a DDHH toward the left with the 6th thread from the LS.

10 Set aside the first thread on both sides; they will be finished later. Thread 5 crystals onto the 5th thread from the RS. Taking care to use the thread with the beads first, arrange the other threads upward as shown in the photo. Using your RH, take the 1st thread from the RS and, using your

LH, make a DDHH toward the right with the 5th thread (the thread with 5 crystals). Thread 6 crystals onto the 4th thread from the RS. Using your RH, take the 1st thread from the RS and, using your LH, make a DDHH toward the right with the 4th thread (the thread with 6 crystals). Thread 7 crystals onto the 3rd thread from the RS. Using your RH, take the 1st thread from the RS and, using your LH, make a DDHH toward the right with the 3rd thread (the thread with 7 crystals). Thread 8 crystals onto the 2nd thread from the RS. Using your RH, take the 1st thread from the RS and, using your LH, make a DDHH toward the right with the 2nd thread (the thread with 8 crystals). Repeat this step on the LS, reversing shaping.

11 Using your LH, take the 5th thread from the RS and, using your RH, make a DDHH toward the left with the 5th, 4th, 3rd, 2nd, and 1st threads from the LS.

Completing the Earrings

12 Using your RH, take the 5th thread from the RS and, using LH, make a DDHH to the right with the 4th, 3rd, 2nd, and 1st threads from the RS.

13 Using your RH, take the 5th thread from the LS and make a DDHH to the right with the 5th, 4th, 3rd, 2nd, and 1st threads from the RS. Using your LH, take the 5th thread from the LS and make a DDHH to the left with the 4th, 3rd, 2nd, and 1st threads from the LS.

14 Using your LH, take the 5th thread from the RS. Using your RH, make a DDHH to the left with the 5th, 4th, 3rd, and 2nd threads from the LS. Using your RH, take the 5th thread from the RS and, using your LH, make a DDHH to the right with the 4th, 3rd, and 2nd threads from the RS.

15 Using your RH, take the 3rd thread from the LS and, using your LH, make a DDHH to the right with the 3rd, 2nd, and 1st threads from the RS. Using your LH, take the 3rd thread from the LS, and using your RH, make a DDHH to the left with threads 2 and 1 from the left.

16 Using your LH, take the 2nd thread from the RS and, using your RH, make a DDHH to the left with the 2nd and 1st threads from the LS. Using your RH, take the 2nd thread from the RS and, using your LH, make a DDHH to the right with the 1st thread from the right.

17 Using your LH, take the 1st thread from the RS and, using your RH, make a DDHH toward the left with the 1st thread from the LS.

18 Using your LH, take the 1st thread from the RS and, using your RH, make a DDHH toward the left with 4 threads.

19 Using your RH, take the 1st thread from the LS and, using your LH, make a DDHH toward the right with 5 threads.

20 Secure all the threads on the back of the work and seal them (see page 9). Make another earring in the same way.

Variation

Spiral Bracelet

Make a bracelet to match the earrings on pages 63–66 using the same techniques.

You Will Need:

Four 78¾ in. (200cm) lengths of ¹⁄₆₄ in. (0.5mm) blue waxed thread

Twelve silver jump rings

One silver clasp

189 crystal beads, ¹⁄₁₆ in. (2mm) in diameter

Types of Knot:

DDHH: Diagonal double half hitch

RLH + HHEC: Reverse lark's head plus half hitch each cord

Abbreviations:

LH: Left hand

LS: Left-hand side

RH: Right hand

RS: Right-hand side

Difficulty Rating:

Easy

Size:

Knotted section 6⅜ in. (16cm) long, length of bracelet is adjustable

1 Lay 1 length of thread horizontally. Add 3 threads in the center using a RLH + HHEC in the center of each one.

2 Using your LH, take the 1st thread from the RS and, using your RH, make a DDHH toward the left with all the threads.

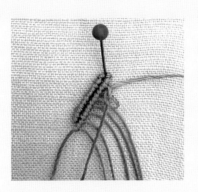

3 Using your LH, take the 1st thread from the RS and, using your RH, make a DDHH toward the left with all the threads. Repeat 18 more times.

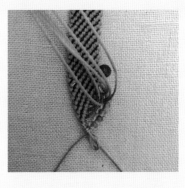

4 Thread 6 beads onto the 1st thread on the RS. Arrange all the threads to the left as shown in the photo. Using your RH, take the 1st thread from the LS and make DDHH toward the right with the 1st thread.

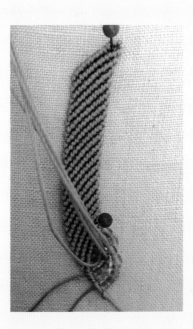

5 Thread 7 beads onto the 2nd thread from the RS. Using your RH, take the 1st thread from the LS and make DDHH toward the right with the 2nd thread (the thread with 7 beads). Continue in the same way by threading 8 beads onto the 3rd thread, 9 beads onto the 4th thread, 10 beads onto the 5th thread, 11 beads onto the 6th thread, and 12 beads onto the 7th thread.

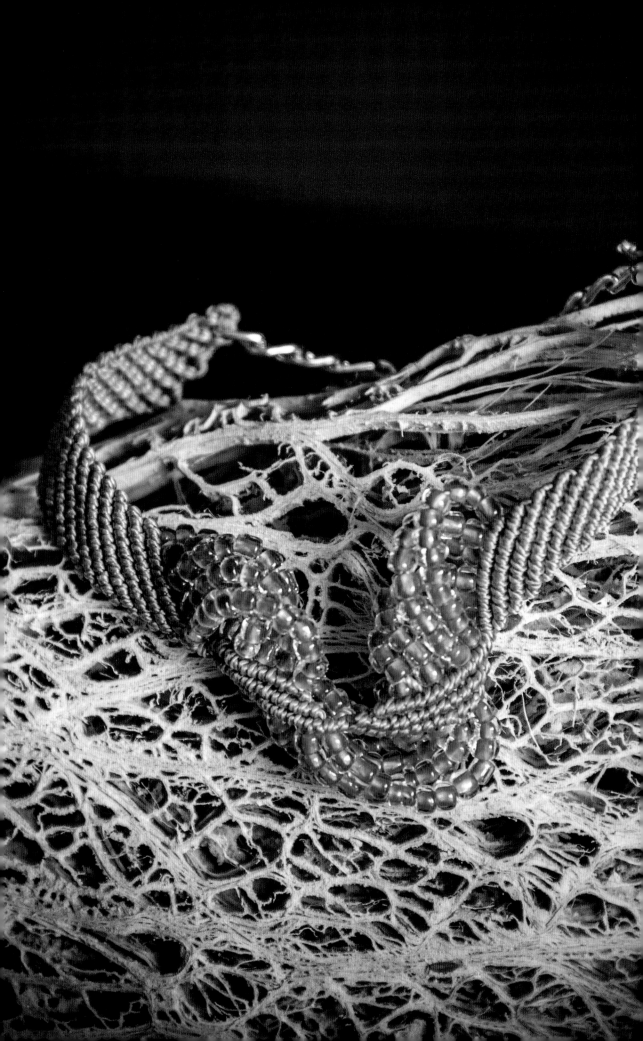

6 Using your RH, take the 1st thread from the LS and make DDHH toward the right with all the threads. Repeat twice more.

7 Thread 6 beads onto the 1st thread from the LS. Arrange all the threads to the left as shown in the photo. Using your LH, take the 1st thread from the RS and, using your RH, make a DDHH toward the left with the 1st thread (the thread with 6 beads). Continue in the same way by threading 7 beads onto the 2nd thread, 8 beads onto the 3rd thread, 9 beads onto the 4th thread, 10 beads onto the 5th thread, 11 beads onto the 6th thread, and 12 beads onto the 7th thread.

8 Using your LH, take the 1st thread from the RS and, using your RH, make a DDHH toward the left with all the threads.

9 Using your LH, take the 1st thread from the RS and, using your RH, make a DDHH toward the left with all the threads. Repeat once more.

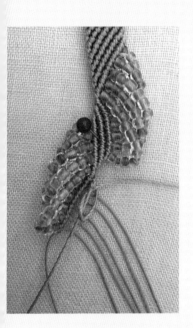

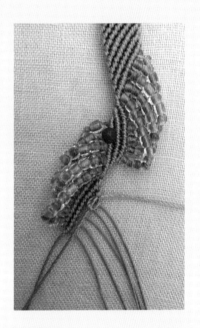

10 Repeat steps 4 and 5.

11 Using your RH, take the 1st thread from the LS and make DDHH toward the right with all the threads. Repeat 19 more times.

12 Secure the threads at the back of the work and seal the ends (see page 9). Using chain nose pliers, attach 5 jump rings and the clasp to one end of the bracelet and 7 silver jump rings to the other end of the bracelet.

Love Hearts Bracelet

Two sizes of heart-shaped hematite beads add a sophisticated sparkle to this intricate bracelet. Remember to use pins to secure the threads as you work to help to position the half hitch and square knots and beads.

You Will Need:

Eight 40 in. (1m) lengths of $\frac{1}{32}$ in. (1mm) bordeaux waxed thread

Eight small $\frac{1}{4}$ in. (6mm) hematite heart-shaped beads

Twenty large $\frac{5}{16}$ in. (8mm) hematite heart-shaped beads

Three silver jump rings

One silver clasp

Types of Knot:

ASK: Alternative square knot

DDHH: Diagonal double half hitch

HH: Half hitch

RDHH: Reverse double half hitch

RLH: Reverse lark's head

RLH + HH: Reverse lark's head plus half hitch

SK: Square knot

Abbreviations:

LH: Left hand

LS: Left-hand side

RH: Right hand

RS: Right-hand side

Difficulty Rating:

Advanced

Size:

Knotted section 7 in. (18cm) long, length of bracelet is adjustable

Starting the Bracelet

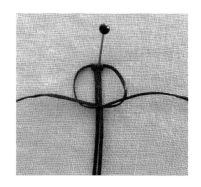

1 Take 1 length of thread and lay it horizontally. Add a 2nd thread in the center using a RLH and make a SK with the 4 threads.

2 Add a thread with a RLH + HH on the RS. Repeat on the LS.

3 Using your LH, take the 5th thread from the left and make DDHH to the left with the 4th, 3rd, 2nd, and 1st threads from the LS.

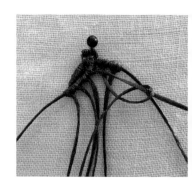

4 Using your RH, take the 4th thread from the right and make DDHH to the right with the 3rd, 2nd, and 1st threads from the RS.

Adding the Beads

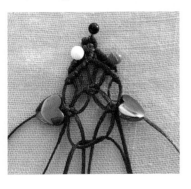

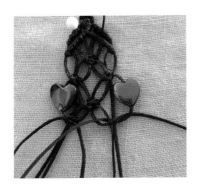

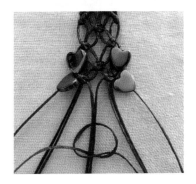

5 Make a SK with the 4 central threads. Divide the threads into 2 groups of 4 threads, and use to make a SK on both sides. Thread a large bead onto the external thread on each side. Make a SK with the 4 central threads.

6 Make a SK both sides.

7 Thread a large bead onto the external thread on each side. Add a new thread with a SK over the 2 central threads.

8 Make a SK on both sides.

9 Thread 2 large beads onto the external thread on each side, positioning them tip-to-tip. Make a SK on each side with the 4 right-hand threads and the 4 left-hand threads without using the external threads.

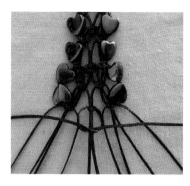

10 Make a SK both sides. Add a new thread in the center, and use it to make a SK around the 2 central threads.

11 Add a new thread to the outside threads on both sides and secure with a RLH. Thread a small bead onto each of the external threads and make a SK with the 4 central threads on both sides.

12 Make a SK with the 4 threads on both sides.

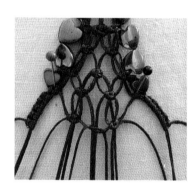

13 With 1st thread on LS, make 5 RDHH around the 2 threads added in step 11. Repeat on RS, reversing shaping. There are 10 central threads. Make a SK with 4 threads on both sides (do not use the 2 central threads). Make a SK using the 2 central threads.

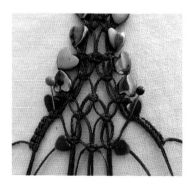

14 Thread a small bead onto both sides of the central section as shown in the photo.

15 With the 1st thread on the LS make 13 RDHH around the 2 threads added in step 11 and the thread to which you have

just added the small bead. There are 8 central threads. Make a SK with the 4 threads on both sides. Thread a large bead onto the 2 central threads of each SK and join with a DHH.

16 Thread 2 large beads as shown in the photo and make a SK with the 4 threads on both sides.

17 Thread a small bead onto the 4th thread from the RS and 4th thread from the LS. On both sides, make a SK using 3 of the threads from the previous SK and the thread where you have threaded the heart.

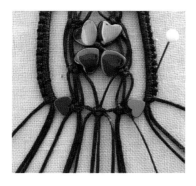

18 Make a SK using the 4 central threads.

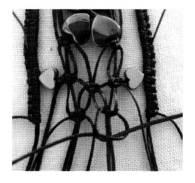

19 Make a SK with the 4 central threads on both sides.

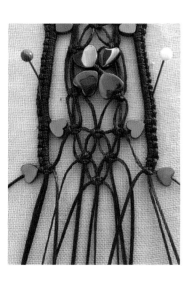

20 Make a SK with the 4 central threads. Make a SK with the 4 exterior threads on both sides. Thread a small bead onto the exterior thread on each side as shown in the photo.

21 With your LH, use the exterior right-hand thread to make DHH with 1 thread. Repeat using your RH on the LS, reversing shaping.

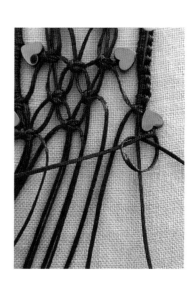

Completing the Bracelet

22 Make SK with the 4 exterior threads on both sides.

23 Take 2 threads from the central SK and 2 threads to the right and 2 to the left of the previous SK to the back of the work and arrange

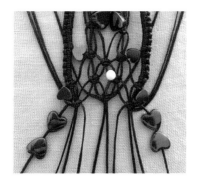

them out of the way. When you have finished making the bracelet, these threads must be sewn to the back, trimmed, and sealed (see page 9). Thread 2 large beads on the exterior threads on each side as shown in the photo.

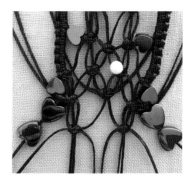

24 Make a SK with the 4 threads on both sides.

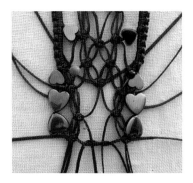

25 Make a SK with the 4 threads on both sides. Make a 3rd SK using the 2 central threads and the threads to their immediate left and right.

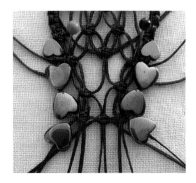

26 Take the 4th threads from the left and right to the back of the work. (At the end, these threads must be finished as described in step 23.) Thread a large bead onto the external threads on both sides.

27 Make a SK with the 4 RH threads. Repeat with the 4 LH threads. Make a SK with the 4 central threads.

28 Thread a large bead on the exterior threads on both sides. Make a SK with the 4 RS threads. Repeat with the 4 LS threads.

29 Make a SK with the 4 central threads. With your RH, take the 1st thread on the LS to the right to make a DHH with the 2nd, 3rd, and 4th threads.

30 With your LH, take the 1st thread on the RS to the left to make a DHH with the 2nd, 3rd, and 4th threads. Join the 2 central threads with a DHH.

31 Make a DHH on both sides as in steps 29 and 30. Make a SK with the 4 central threads.

Attaching the Clasp

32 Knot the 2 central threads around the jump ring of the clasp. Sew at the back, trim, and seal (see page 9).

33 Add 2 silver jump rings to the other end of the bracelet using a pair of chain nose pliers. Finish the threads taken to the back in steps 23 and 26.

Two-strand Bracelet

Two contrasting shades of blue are used to make this double bracelet, while beads and a fringed clasp add extra visual interest.

You Will Need:

Three 35½ in. (90cm) lengths of 1/32 in. (1mm) blue waxed thread

One 35½ in. (90cm) length of 1/32 in. (1mm) light blue waxed thread

Four silver jump rings

One silver clasp

Twenty-four smooth hematite oval beads, 3/16 x 3/32 in. (5 x 3mm)

Types of Knot:

AEDHH: Accumulated edge using double half hitch

AHH: Alternative half hitch chain

DHH: Double half hitch

HDHH: Horizontal double half hitch

RDHH: Reverse double half hitch

RLH + HHEC: Reverse lark's head plus half hitch each cord

RLH: Reverse lark's head

SK: Square knot

HKS: Half knot spiral

VDHH: Vertical double half hitch

VRLH + HHEC: Vertical reverse lark's head plus half hitch each cord

Abbreviations:

LH: Left hand

LS: Left-hand side

RH: Right hand

RS: Right-hand side

Difficulty Rating:

Medium

Size:

Knotted section 5 7/8 in. (15cm) long, length of bracelet is adjustable

Making the First Strand

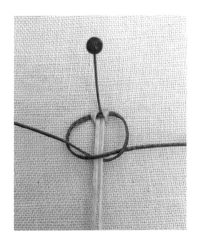

1 Lay 1 length of blue thread horizontally. Add the light blue thread in the center using a RLH in the center. Make a SK with the dark blue thread.

2 Add 1 blue thread with a SK. Make 4 SK.

3 Make 9 SK with the blue thread on the left and the light blue thread on the right. Do not work the 2 blue threads on the RS.

4 Using your RH, take the 1st thread from the LS and make DDHH to the right with the 2nd, 3rd, and 4th threads.

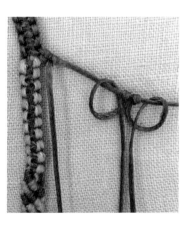

5 Using your RH, take the 1st thread from the LS and make DDHH to the right with the 2nd, 3rd, and 4th threads. Repeat 4 times more.

6 Make HKS for ¾ in. (2cm). Make 7 AHH.

7 Make RDHH until your work measures 4¾ in. (12cm) from the beginning of step 3.

8 Using your RH, take the 1st blue thread from the RS and make DHH with the 2nd blue thread.

Adding the Second Strand

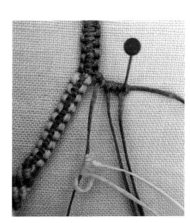

9 Add 1 blue thread with a RLH + HHEC.

10 Add 1 light blue thread to the 1st blue thread from the LS using a VRLH + HHEC.

11 Using your LH, take the 2nd blue thread from the LS and, using RH, make a VDHH with the light blue thread.

12 Using your LH, take the 3rd blue thread from the LS and, using your RH, make a VDHH with the light blue thread.

Completing the Bracelet

13 Using your LH, take the 4th blue thread from the LS, and using your RH, make a VDHH with the light blue thread.

14 Repeat steps 11 to 13 with the 2nd light blue thread.

15 Thread a bead onto the 1st light blue thread on the RS. Using your RH, take the 1st thread from the LS and make DDHH to the right with the 2nd and 3rd threads.

16 Holding the 1st and 3rd threads from the LS together in your RH, make DDHH to the right with the 4th thread.

17 Using your RH, take one of the two threads worked in previous step and make DHH to the right with the other thread.

18 Thread a bead on the 1st blue thread on the LS. Make a VDHH with the light blue thread around the 2nd and 3rd blue threads. Make a DHH with the 1st blue thread from the LS around the 4th blue thread.

19 Make VDHH, with the light blue thread around the 3rd and 4th blue threads.

20 Using your LH, take the 1st blue thread from the LS and, using your RH, make a vertical DHH with the 1st light blue thread on the RS. Repeat step 11, then repeat steps

12 to 17 eight times. Using your RH, take the 1st blue thread from the RS and make AEDHH with all the blue threads. Secure the light blue threads on both sides at the back of the work and seal the ends (see page 9). Make sure that the threads on both sides are aligned then make 6 SK.

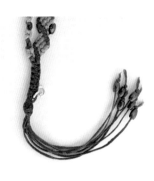

21 Tie a knot with all the threads and add 2 jump rings using chain nose pliers. Thread a bead onto each thread and knot. Add 2 jump rings and the clasp to the other end of the bracelet.

Tiger's Eye Earrings

Half hitch, square, and lark's head knots tied in a combination of beige and brown threads provide the perfect frame for the tiger's eye beads in these earrings.

You Will Need:

Four 27½ in. (70 cm) lengths ¹/₃₂ in. (1mm) Linhasita brown waxed thread

Six 27½ in. (70 cm) lengths ¹/₃₂ in. (1mm) Linhasita beige waxed thread

Eight tiger's eye round beads, ¼ in. (6mm) in diameter

Two copper earwires

Types of Knot:

AEDHH: Accumulated edge using double half hitches

DHH: Double half hitch

DDHH: Diagonal double half hitch

HDHH: Horizontal double half hitch

LH: Lark's head

RDHH: Reverse double half hitch

RLH + HHEC: Reverse lark's head plus half hitch each cord

RLH: Reverse lark's head

SK: Square knot

VDHH: Vertical double half hitch

VRLH + HHEC: Vertical Reverse lark's head plus half hitch each cord

Abbreviations:

LH: Left hand

LS: Left-hand side

RH: Right hand

RS: Right-hand side

Difficulty Rating:

Advanced

Size:

2¾ in. (7cm) long

Starting the Earrings

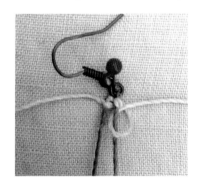

1 Thread a brown thread into an earwire. Add a beige thread with a VDHH in the center around the brown thread on one side of the earwire. With the beige thread, make a VDHH around the brown thread on the other side of the earwire.

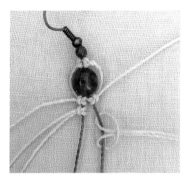

2 Thread 1 bead onto both ends of the brown thread. With the beige thread, make a RDHH around the brown thread on both sides. Add a new beige thread with your LH on both sides.

3 Using your LH, take the brown thread from the LS and, using your RH, make a DDHH to the left with the beige 1st, 2nd, and 3rd threads. Repeat using your RH and the beige 1st, 2nd, and 3rd threads, reversing shaping.

4 Add a new brown thread with a SK around the 2 central beige threads.

5 Using your LH, take the brown thread from the LS and, using your RH, make a DDHH to the left with the 1st beige thread.

6 Using your RH, take the 1st brown thread from the LS and, using your LH, make a DDHH to the left with the 1st beige thread. Repeat on the RS, reversing shaping.

7 Arrange the 2 central beige threads at the back of the work; they will not be used for the time being. Using your LH, take the 1st brown thread from RS and make a DDHH to the left with the brown and beige threads. Repeat on the LS, reversing shaping.

8 With your LH, take the 4th thread from the RS to the left to make a DHH with the 4th thread from the LS.

9 Using your LH, take the brown thread from the LS and, using your RH, make a DDHH to the left with the 1st beige thread.

10 Using your RH, take the 1st brown thread from the LS and, using your LH, make a DDHH to the left with the 1st beige thread.

11 Using your LH, take the 2nd brown thread from the LS and, using your RH, make a DDHH to the left with the 1st beige thread.

12 With your LH, take the 2nd brown thread from the LS to the left to make a DHH with the 1st brown thread from the LS. Repeat steps 9 to 12 on the RS, reversing shaping.

13 Using your LH, take the brown thread on the LS and, using your RH, make a DDHH to

the left with the 1st beige thread. Using your RH, take the 1st brown thread from the LS and, using your LH, make a DDHH to the left with the 1st beige thread. Using your RH, take the 2nd brown thread from the LS and, using your LH, make a DDHH to the right with the 2nd beige thread. Repeat on RS, reversing shaping.

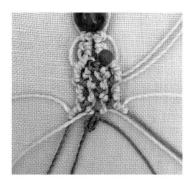

14 With your LH, take the 2nd brown thread from the RS to the left to make a DHH with the 2nd brown thread from the LS.

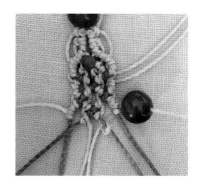

15 Thread a bead onto the 1st beige thread on the RS. Using your LH, take the 2nd brown thread from the LS and, using your RH, make a DDHH to the left with the nearest beige thread. Repeat on the RS, reversing shaping.

16 With your LH, take the 1st brown thread from the RS to the left to make a DHH with the 2nd brown thread from the RS.

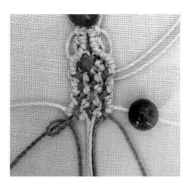

17 With your LH, take the 2nd brown thread from the LS to the left to make a DHH with the 1st brown thread from the LS.

18 Using your RH, take the 1st beige thread from the LS and, using your LH, make a DHH knot to the right with the 1st brown thread.

19 Holding the 1st beige and brown threads together in your RH, and working from the LS using your LH, make a DDHH to the right with the 2nd brown thread.

20 Holding the 1st beige and the 1st and 2nd brown threads together in your RH, and working from the LS using your LH, make a DDHH to the right with the 1st beige thread.

21 Holding a beige and a brown thread in your RH, make a DDHH to the right with a brown thread using your LH. Holding a beige thread in your RH, and using your LH, make a DHH to the right with a brown thread.

22 Using your RH, take the 1st beige thread from the LS and, using your LH, make a DDHH to the right with the 1st and 2nd brown threads.

Completing the Earrings

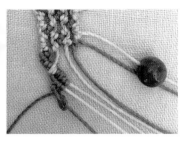

23 Using your RH, take the 1st brown thread from the LS and, using your LH, make a DDHH to the right with the 2nd brown thread.

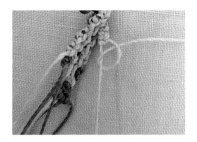

24 Make 13 RDHH with the two beige threads that have not been worked before.

25 Work the four central threads as follows: Using your RH, take the 1st beige thread from the LS and, using your LH, make a DDHH to the right with the 2nd and 3rd brown threads.

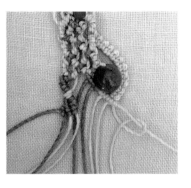

26 Using your RH, take the diagonal beige thread and, using your LH, make a DDHH to the right with the beige thread holding the bead. Repeat, making the DDHH to the right with 2 beige threads.

27 Using your RH, take the 1st brown thread from the LS and, using your LH, make a DDHH to the right with the 2nd, 3rd, and 4th threads.

28 With your LH, take the 1st beige thread from the RS to the left and, using your RH, make a DHH with the 2nd beige thread from the RS.

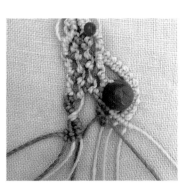

29 Using your RH, take the 1st brown thread from the LS and, using your LH, make a DDHH to the right with the 2nd and 3rd beige threads.

30 Using your RH, take the 4th beige thread from the LS and, using your LH, make a DDHH to the right with the 2 central beige threads.

31 Using your RH, take the 3rd beige thread from the LS and, using your LH, make a DDHH to the right with the 2 central beige threads.

32 Using your RH, take the 2nd brown thread from the LS and, using your LH, make a DDHH to the right with the 2 central beige threads.

33 Using your RH, take the 1st brown thread from the LS and, using your LH, make a DDHH to the right with the 2 central beige threads.

34 Thread a bead onto the 2nd beige thread on the LS. With your LH, take the 2nd beige thread from the RS to the left and, using your RH, make AEDHH with 6 threads.

35 With your LH, take the 6 threads just worked and, using your RH, make a DDHH to the left with the beige thread holding the bead.

36 Thread 1 bead onto 1 of the brown threads just worked. With your LH, take the 6 threads just worked and, using your RH, make a DDHH to the left with the beige, brown, beige, and beige threads.

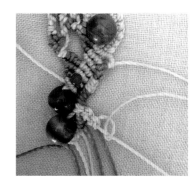

37 With your LH, take a brown thread and, using your RH, make a DDHH to the left with the brown thread with the bead. Make 4 RDHH with 2 beige threads.

38 Make 4 RDHH with 2 brown threads. Make 4 RDHH with 2 beige threads.

39 Using your RH, take the 1st brown thread from the RS and, using your LH, make a DDHH to the right with the 2nd beige thread from the RS.

40 Using your RH, take the 2nd beige thread from the LS and, with your LH, make a DDHH to the right with the brown, beige, and brown threads. Finish the threads (see page 9). Make another earring, reversing the shaping so it is symmetrical.

Entwined Coral Bracelet

A framework of knotted waxed thread is embellished with heart-shaped hematite beads and then entwined with a coil of coral beads. The coral beads are threaded through square knot buttons.

You Will Need:

Five 59 in. (150 cm) lengths of $\frac{1}{32}$ in. (1mm) orange waxed thread

Sixteen $\frac{1}{4}$ in. (6mm) heart-shaped hematite beads

Thirty-four faceted round coral-colored crystal beads, $\frac{5}{32}$ in. (4mm) in diameter

Fifteen silver jump rings

One silver clasp

Two $\frac{3}{4}$ in. (2cm) silver-colored ribbon clamps

Types of Knot:

AHH: Alternative half hitch

HDHH: Horizontal double half hitch

RLH + HHEC: Reverse lark's head plus half hitch each cord

SK: Square knot

SKB: Square knot button

Abbreviations:

LH: Left hand

LS: Left-hand side

RH: Right hand

RS: Right-hand side

Difficulty Rating:

Easy

Size:

Knotted section 4⅞ in. (12.5cm) long, length of bracelet is adjustable

Starting the Bracelet

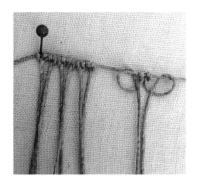

1 Position 1 length of thread horizontally. Add 4 threads in the center using a RLH + HHEC.

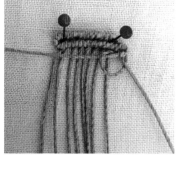

2 Using your RH, take the 1st thread from the LS and make HDHH to the right with 9 threads. Using your LH, take the 1st thread from RS and make HDHH to the left with 9 threads. Repeat once more.

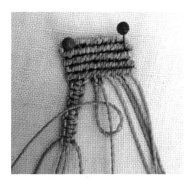

3 Make 7 SK with 4 threads on the LS. Make 1 AHH with 2 central threads.

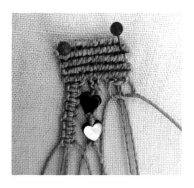

4 Thread 1 hematite bead onto the central thread and make 1 AHH. Repeat once. Make 7 SK with the 4 threads on the RS.

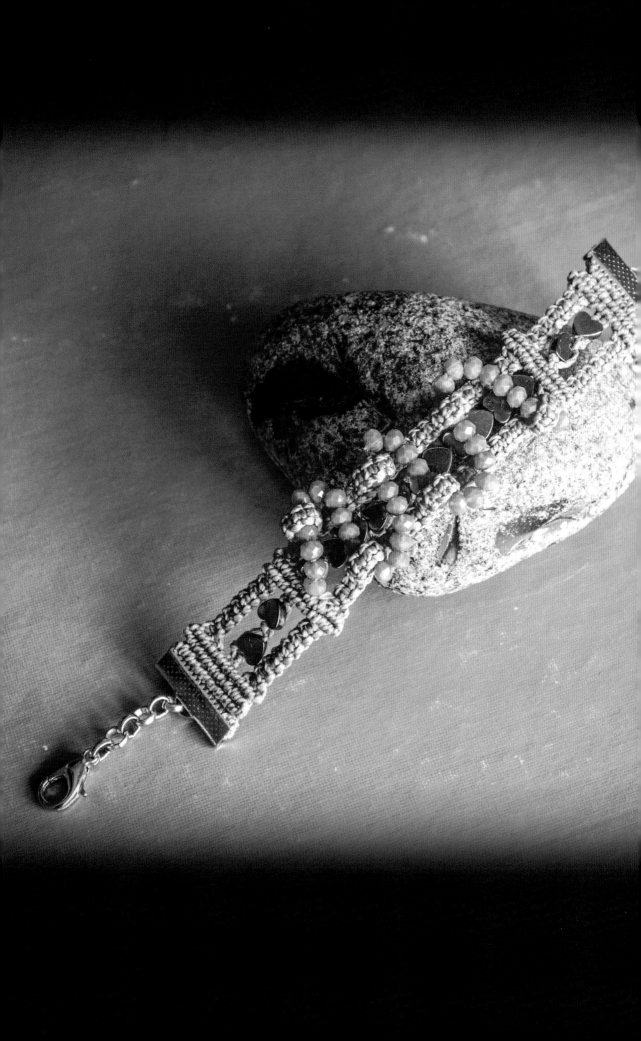

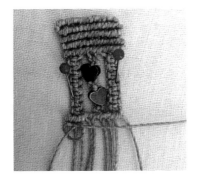

5 Using your LH, take the 1st thread from the RS and make HDHH to the left with 9 threads.

6 Using your RH, take the 1st thread from the LS and make HDHH to the right with 9 threads.

7 Make 4 SK with the 4 threads on the LS.

Adding Square Knot Buttons

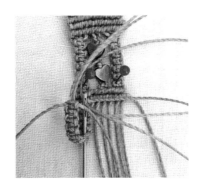
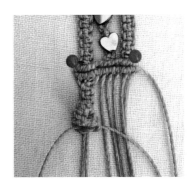

8 Insert a tapestry needle after the 4th SK and make 1 SK around the needle. Make 6 more SK.

9 Use the needle to pass the 2 central threads of the SK through the point where you inserted the needle. (You have made 1 SKB.)

10 Make 5 SK with the 4 threads on the LS.

11 Make 1 SKB (repeat steps 8 and 9), 10 SK, 1 SKB, 1 SK. Thread 12 hematite beads onto 1 central thread and 34 crystal beads onto the other central thread. Make 2 SK with the 4 threads on the RS. Make 1 SKB, 6 SK, 1 SKB, 7 SK, 1 SKB, 6 SK. Insert the thread holding the beads inside the SKBs, as shown in the photo.

12 Repeat step 6, then steps 5, 4, 3, and 2, reversing shaping. Make 1 HDHH with all the threads.

13 Finish the threads at the back of the work (see page 9). Use a pair of chain nose pliers to attach a silver-colored ribbon clamp to each end of the bracelet. Then use the pliers to join 7 silver jump rings and 1 silver clasp to 1 end of the bracelet. Add 8 silver jump rings to the other end of the bracelet.

Golden Crystal Choker

Clusters of crystal and gold-colored beads surrounded with half hitch knots create this choker necklace. You can repeat the clusters as many times as you like to make the choker the perfect length for you to wear.

You Will Need:

Four 4½ yd. (4m) lengths of 1mm beige waxed thread

One 19⅝ in. (50cm) length of 1mm beige waxed thread

One 21⅝ in. (55cm) length of 1mm beige waxed thread

Sixty-six faceted round crystals, ³⁄₁₆ in. (5mm) in diameter

Seventy-seven round gold-colored beads, ¹⁄₁₆ in. (2mm) in diameter

Types of Knot:

DHH: Double half hitch

DDHH: Diagonal double half hitch

HDHH: Horizontal double half hitch

RDHH: Reverse double half hitch

RLH + HH: Reverse lark's head plus half hitch

SK: Square knot

Abbreviations:

LH: Left hand

LS: Left-hand side

RH: Right hand

RS: Right-hand side

Difficulty Rating:

Medium

Size:

Knotted section 9½ in. (24cm) long, length of choker is adjustable

Starting the Choker

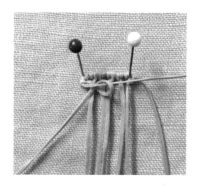

1 Lay one 4½ yd. (4m) length of thread horizontally. Add three 4½ yd (4m) lengths of thread in the center using a RLH + HH with each one. Using your RH, take the 1st thread from the LS and make HDHH to the right with all 7 threads.

2 Using your LH, take the 1st thread on the RS and make HDHH to the left with all 7 threads.

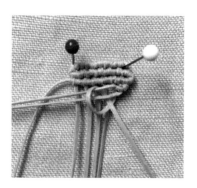

3 Using your LH, take the 1st thread on the RS and make HDHH to the left with 1 thread. Using your LH and the 2 threads just worked, make HDHH to the left with 1 thread.

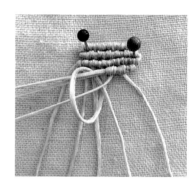

4 Using your LH and the 3 threads just worked, make HDHH to the left with 1 thread.

5 Using these 4 threads make HDHH to the left with the 3rd, 2nd, and 1st threads.

6 With one of the outermost 4 threads, make 8 RDHH on the 3 remaining threads.

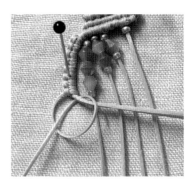

7 Thread 1 bead onto 1st thread on RS; 1 bead, 1 crystal, 1 bead onto the 2nd thread; 1 bead, 2 crystals, 1 bead onto the 3rd thread; 1 bead, 3 crystals, 1 bead onto 4th thread. Use 1 of the 4 threads on the LS to make a DHH to the right around the 3 other threads.

8 Make a DHH to the right with the 2nd, 3rd, and 4th threads around the 3 remaining threads.

9 With 1 of the 3 threads grouped together, make a DHH to the right, repeat with 1 of the 2 remaining threads. With the last thread, make 1 DHH to the right.

10 Using your LH, take the 1st thread from the RS and make DDHH to the left with all 7 threads.

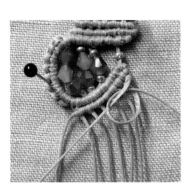

11 Using your LH, take the 1st thread from the RS and make DDHH to the left with all 7 threads. Repeat once more.

12 Repeat steps 3 to 11 on the other side of the cluster of beads, reversing the shaping, until you have a total of 11 motifs. Check the choker for size, and if you want it longer, make more motifs as desired.

13 Make 3 bars of DDHH. Add a 19½ in. (50cm) thread to the other end of the necklace. Place the threads so they face in opposite directions and, with a new 21½ in. (55cm) thread, make a sliding closure (see page 12).

Golden Crystal Bracelet

Clusters of sparkling beads contrast with half hitch knots made in a neutral-colored waxed thread for this elegant bracelet.

You Will Need:

Four 74⅞ in. (190cm) lengths of ¹⁄₃₂ in. (1mm) beige waxed thread

Two 19⅝ in. (50cm) lengths of ¹⁄₃₂ in. (1mm) beige waxed thread

Twenty ³⁄₁₆ in. (5mm) faceted round crystals

Fourteen ¹⁄₁₆ in. (2mm) gold-colored round metal beads

Types of Knot:

AEDHH: Accumulated edge using double half hitches

DDHH: Diagonal double half hitch

DHH: Double half hitch

HDHH: Horizontal double half hitch

RDHH: Reverse double half hitch

RLH + HHEC: Reverse lark's head plus half hitch each cord

SK: Square knot

Abbreviations:

LH: Left hand

LS: Left-hand side

RH: Right hand

RS: Right-hand side

Difficulty Rating:

Medium

Size:

Knotted section 5⅞ in. (15cm) long, length of bracelet is adjustable

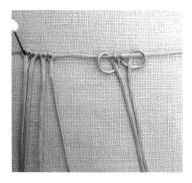

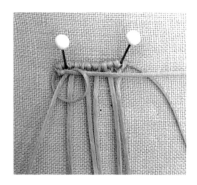

1 Position a 74⅞ in. (190cm) thread horizontally. Add three 74⅞ in. (190cm) threads in the center using RLH + HHEC.

2 Using your RH, take the 1st thread from the LS and make a HDHH toward the right with all 7 threads. Using your LH, take

the 1st thread from the RS and make a HDHH toward the left with all 7 threads. Using your RH, take the 1st thread from the LS and make a HDHH toward the right with all 7 threads.

3 Using your LH, take the 4th thread from the LS and make a DDHH toward the left with 1 thread. Holding these 2 threads together in your LH, make a DDHH toward the left with 1 thread. Holding these 3 threads as before, make a DDHH toward the left with 1 thread.

4 Using your LH, take 1st thread from the LS and make 4 RDHH on the 3 threads being held together. Repeat steps 3 and 4 on the RS, reversing shaping.

5 Make a SK using the 1st thread from both sides. Thread 1 crystal onto the 1st threads on both sides. Make a SK.

6 Using your LH, take the 1st thread from the LS and make 6 RDHH on the 3 threads next to it. Repeat on the RS, reversing shaping.

7 Make a SK using the 1st thread on both sides. Insert 1 crystal on the threads on both sides. Make a SK. Using your LH, take the 1st thread from the RS and make a DDHH toward the left with all 7 threads.

8 Using your LH, take the 1st thread from the RS and make a DDHH toward the left with all 7 threads. Repeat these knots once more.

9 Using your LH, take the 1st thread from the RS and make a DDHH toward the left with the

2nd and 3rd threads. Holding the 1st and the 3rd threads together in your LH, make a DDHH toward the left with 1 thread. Holding the 1st, 3rd, and 4th threads together in your LH, make a DDHH toward the left with 1 thread. Repeat the final DDHH twice more.

10 Using your LH, take the 1st thread from the LS and make 8 RDHH on the 3 threads being held together. Insert beads as shown in the photo.

11 Holding the 3 threads from the LS together in your RH, make a DDHH toward the right with

the thread with 3 crystals, the thread with 2 crystals, and then the thread with 1 crystal. Using your RH, take 2 threads from the LS and make a DDHH toward the right with 1 thread. Using your RH, take the 1 thread from the LS and make a DDHH toward the right with 1 thread.

12 Using your RH, take the 1 thread from the OLS and make a DDHH toward the right with the thread with 1 gold bead. Using your LH, take the 1st thread from the RS and make a DDHH toward the left with all 7 threads.

13 Using your LH, take the 1st thread from the RS and make a DDHH toward the left with all 7 threads. Repeat these knots once more.

14 Using your RH, take the 1st thread from the LS and make a DDHH toward the right with the 2nd and 3rd threads. Holding the 1st and the 3rd threads together in your RH, make a DDHH toward the right with 1 thread. Holding the 1st, 3rd, and 4th threads together in your RH, make a DDHH toward right with 1 thread. Repeat the final DDHH twice more.

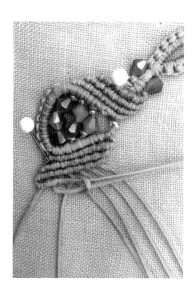

15 Using your RH, take the 1st thread from the RS and make 8 RDHH on the 3 threads being held together. Insert beads as shown in the photo.

16 Using your LH, take the 3 threads being held together from the RS and make a DDHH

toward the left with the thread with 3 crystals, the thread with 2 crystals, and then the thread with 1 crystal. Using your LH, take 2 threads from RS and make a DDHH toward the left with 1 thread. Using your LH, take the 1 thread from RS and make a DDHH toward the left with 1 thread.

17 Using your LH, take the 1 thread from RS and make a DDHH toward the left with the thread with 1 gold bead. Using your RH, take the 1st thread from LS and make a DDHH toward the right with all 7 threads. Repeat the final DDHH twice more.

Completing the Bracelet

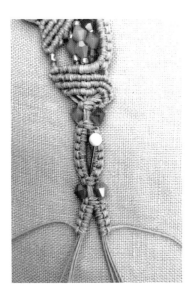

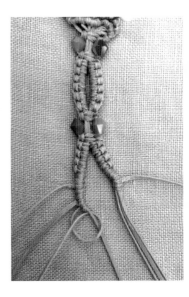

18 Repeat steps 5 to 8. Insert 1 crystal on the threads on both sides. Make a SK. Using your LH, take the 1st thread from LS and make 4 RDHH on the 3 threads being held together. Repeat on the RS, reversing shaping.

19 Using your RH, take 1st thread from the LS and make a DDHH toward the right on the 3 threads held together. Using your LH, take thread just used and make a DDHH toward the left on the 3 threads held together. Repeat on the RS, reversing shaping.

20 Using your RH, take 2 threads from the LS and make a DDHH toward the right with 1 thread. Using your RH, take the 1 thread from the LS and make a DDHH toward the right with 1 thread. Repeat on the RS, reversing shaping.

21 Using your LH, take the 1st thread from the RS and make a DDHH toward the left with all 7 threads. Using your RH, take the 1st thread from the LS and make a DDHH toward the right with all 7 threads. Repeat this step.

22 Sew all the threads except the 2 central ones to the back of the work, trim, and seal (see page 9). Add a 19⅝ in. (50cm) thread to the other end of the bracelet. Make a sliding closure (see page 12) using another 19⅝ in. (50cm) thread and 5 SK. Secure the ends on the back, trim, and seal them as before.

Shades of Silver Bracelet

A dark gray thread complements the sheen of the hexagonal and olive-shaped hematite beads used to decorate this elegant bracelet. The design uses a combination of different half hitch knots.

You Will Need:

Four 59 in. (150cm) lengths of $\frac{1}{32}$ in. (1mm) dark gray waxed thread

Two 11$\frac{7}{8}$ in. (30cm) lengths of $\frac{1}{32}$ in. (1mm) dark gray waxed thread

Four hematite olive-shaped beads, $\frac{5}{16}$ x $\frac{3}{16}$ in. (8 x 5mm)

Four hematite hexagonal beads, $\frac{3}{8}$ x $\frac{1}{4}$ in. (9 x 6mm)

Types of Knot:

AHH: Alternative half hitch

DDHH: Diagonal double half hitch

DHH: Double half hitch

RDHH: Reverse double half hitch

RLH: Reverse lark's head

SK: Square knot

Abbreviations:

LH: Left hand

LS: Left-hand side

RH: Right hand

RS: Right-hand side

Difficulty Rating:

Medium

Size:

Knotted section 6$\frac{3}{8}$ in. (16cm) long, length of bracelet is adjustable

Starting the Bracelet

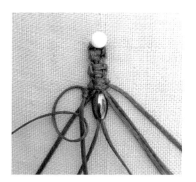

1 Position a 59 in. (150cm) thread horizontally. Add a 59 in. (150cm) thread in the center using a RLH, make 1 SK. Add a 59 in. (150cm) thread in the center using a SK. Repeat with remaining 59 in. (150cm) thread.

2 Thread an olive-shaped bead onto the 2 central threads. Using your RH, take the 1st thread from LS and, using your LH, make a DDHH to the right with the 2nd, 3rd, and 4th threads. Using your LH, take the 1st thread from RS and, using your RH, make a DDHH to the left with the 2nd, 3rd, 4th, and 5th threads. Using your LH, take the 1st thread from RS and, using your RH, make a DDHH to the left with the 2nd, 3rd, and 4th threads. Using your RH, take the 1st thread from LS and, using your LH, make a DDHH to the right with the 2nd, 3rd, 4th, and 5th threads. Using your RH, take the 1st thread from LS and, using your LH, make a DDHH to the right with the 2nd, 3rd, and 4th threads. Using your LH, take the 1st thread from RS and, using your RH, make a DDHH to the left with the 2nd, 3rd, 4th, and 5th threads.

3 Insert a hexagonal bead onto the 1st thread on both sides. Using your LH, take the 2nd thread from the RS and, using your RH, make a DDHH to the left with the 3rd and 4th threads. Using your RH, take the 2nd thread from the LS and, using your LH, make a DDHH to the right with the 3rd, 4th, and 5th threads. Using your RH, take the 2nd thread from the LS and, using your LH, make a DDHH to the right with the 3rd and 4th threads. Using your LH, take the 2nd thread from the RS and, using your RH, make a DDHH to the left with the the 3rd, 4th, and 5th threads.

4 Using your LH, take the 1st thread from RS and, using your RH, make a DDHH to the left with the 2nd, 3rd, and 4th threads. Using your RH, take the 1st thread from LS and, using your LH, make a DDHH to the right with the 2nd, 3rd, 4th, and 5th threads. Using your RH, take the 1st thread from LS and, using your LH, make a DDHH to the right with the 2nd, 3rd, and 4th threads. Using your LH, take the 1st thread from RS and, using your RH, make a DDHH to the left with the 2nd, 3rd, 4th, and 5th threads. Repeat this step once more. Using your LH, take the 1st thread from RS and, using your RH, make a DDHH to the left with the 2nd, 3rd, and 4th threads. Using your RH, take the 1st thread from LS and, using your LH, make a DDHH to the right with the 2nd, 3rd, 4th, and 5th threads.

5 Using your RH, take the 2nd thread from LS and, using your LH, make 9 RDHH. Repeat on RS, reversing shaping.

6 Using your RH, take the 1st thread from LS and, using your LH, make a DDHH to the right with the 2nd thread. Using your LH, take the 1st thread from RS and, using your RH, make a DDHH to the left with the 2nd and 3rd threads. Using your LH, take the 1st thread from RS and, using your RH, make a DDHH

to the left with the 2nd thread. Using your RH, take the 1st thread from LS and, using your LH, make a DDHH to the right with the 2nd and 3rd threads. Using your RH, take the 1st thread from LS and, using your LH, make a DDHH to the right with the 2nd thread. Using your LH, take the 1st thread from RS and, using your RH, make a DDHH to the left with the 2nd and 3rd threads.

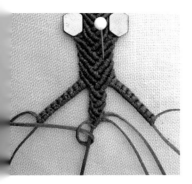

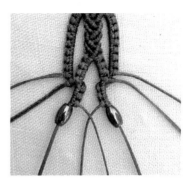

7 Using your RH, take the 4th thread from LS and, using your LH, make 3 RDHH. Repeat on RS, reversing shaping.

8 Using your LH, take the 3rd thread from LS and, using your RH, make a DDHH to the left with the 2nd thread. Repeat on RS, reversing shaping.

9 Make 3 RDHH using 3rd and 4th threads from LS. Repeat on RS, reversing shaping. Thread an olive-shaped bead onto 3rd thread on both sides.

Completing the Bracelet

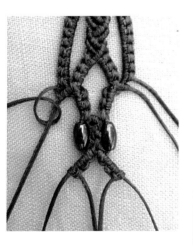

10 Make 3 AHH with the 2 central threads. Using your LH, take the 4th thread from the LS and, using your RH, make 3 RDHH with thread 3. Repeat on the RS, reversing shaping.

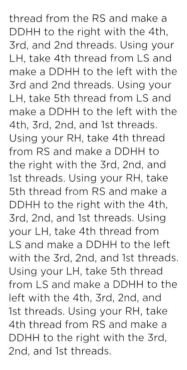

12 Using your LH, take 3rd thread from LS and make a DDHH to the left with the 2nd thread. Repeat on RS, reversing shaping. Repeat step 6, step 8, and then step 7. Using your LH, take 4th thread from LS and make a DDHH to the left with the 3rd, 2nd, and 1st threads. Repeat on RS, reversing shaping. **Using your LH, take 5th thread from LS and make a DDHH to the left with the 4th, 3rd, 2nd, and 1st threads. Using your RH, take 4th thread from RS and make a DDHH to the right with the 3rd, 2nd, and 1st threads. Using your RH, take 5th thread from RS and make a DDHH to the right with the 4th, 3rd, 2nd, and 1st threads. Using your LH, take 4th thread from LS and make a DDHH to the left with the 3rd, 2nd, and 1st threads.** Repeat from ** to **. Thread a hexagonal bead onto the 1st thread on both sides. Using your LH, take 5th thread from LS and, using your RH, make a DDHH to the left with the 4th, 3rd, and 2nd threads. Using your RH, take 4th thread from RS and make a DDHH to the right with the 3rd and 2nd threads. Using your RH, take 5th

thread from the RS and make a DDHH to the right with the 4th, 3rd, and 2nd threads. Using your LH, take 4th thread from LS and make a DDHH to the left with the 3rd and 2nd threads. Using your LH, take 5th thread from LS and make a DDHH to the left with the 4th, 3rd, 2nd, and 1st threads. Using your RH, take 4th thread from RS and make a DDHH to the right with the 3rd, 2nd, and 1st threads. Using your RH, take 5th thread from RS and make a DDHH to the right with the 4th, 3rd, 2nd, and 1st threads. Using your LH, take 4th thread from LS and make a DDHH to the left with the 3rd, 2nd, and 1st threads. Using your LH, take 5th thread from LS and make a DDHH to the left with the 4th, 3rd, 2nd, and 1st threads. Using your RH, take 4th thread from RS and make a DDHH to the right with the 3rd, 2nd, and 1st threads.

13 Thread an olive-shaped bead onto the 2 central threads. Make 1 SK around 6 threads three times. Finish these 6 threads at back of work (see page 9). Make a sliding closure using the 11⅞ in. (30 cm) thread (see page 12).

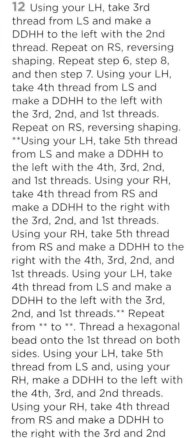

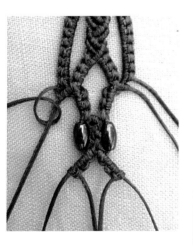

11 Using your RH, take the 2nd thread from the LS and, using your LH, make 6 RDHH. Repeat on the RS, reversing shaping.

Raku Disk Necklace

A dramatic raku-glazed disk turns this simple necklace into a statement piece. The centerpiece is suspended from a cluster of half hitch knots and metallic beads.

You Will Need:

Five 10 ft. (300 cm) lengths of $\frac{1}{32}$ in. (1mm) Linhasita green waxed thread

Five smooth round beads with a metallic antique finish, $\frac{5}{32}$ in. (4mm) in diameter

One raku ceramic disk 2$\frac{3}{8}$ in. (6cm) diameter and with a $\frac{3}{4}$ in. (2cm) diameter hole in the center

One raku ceramic cylinder bead 1$\frac{3}{16}$ in. (3cm) long

One raku ceramic cylinder bead 1 in. (2.5cm) long

Types of Knot:

AEDHH: Accumulated edge using double half hitches

DDHH: Diagonal double half hitch

LHK: Lark's head

RDHH: Reverse double half hitch

SK: Square knot

Abbreviations:

LH: Left hand

LS: Left-hand side

RH: Right hand

RS: Right-hand side

Difficulty Rating:

Advanced

Size:

Knotted section 2$\frac{3}{4}$ in. (7cm) long, length of necklace is adjustable

Starting the Necklace

1 Secure 4 of the 10 ft. (300 cm) lengths of thread through the center of the raku disk with a LHK in the center of the threads. Divide the threads into 2 groups of 4. Make 3 RDHH with 1 of the 4 threads, around the 3 remaining threads on the RS. Repeat on LS, reversing shaping.

2 Add the final 10 ft. (300 cm) length of thread using a SK beneath the 3 RDHH.

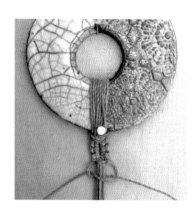

3 Insert a round bead onto the 1st thread on both sides. Holding the 7 central threads together in your RH, and using your LH, make a DDHH toward the right with 1 thread. Repeat using the 6 central threads, then the 5, 4, 3, 2, and 1 central thread to make a DDHH toward the right with 1 thread each time.

4 Holding the same thread in your RH, using your LH, make a DDHH to the right with the thread holding the bead.

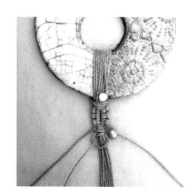

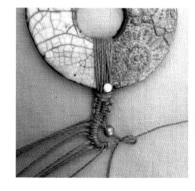

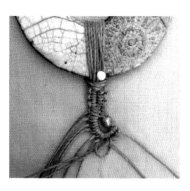  

5 Using your LH, take the 1st thread from RS and, using your RH, make a DDHH to the left with the 2nd and 3rd threads. Holding these 2 threads in LH, and using your RH, make a DDHH to the left with the 4th thread. Don't tie the 2nd thread. Holding these 3

threads together in your LH, and using your RH, make a DDHH to the left with the 5th thread.

6 Holding these 3 threads in LH, and using your RH, make a DDHH to the left with the 6th thread. Don't tie the 5th thread.

7 Holding these 4 threads together in LH, and using your RH, make a DDHH to the left with the 7th thread. Holding these 4 threads together in LH, and using your RH, make a DDHH to the left with the 8th thread. Don't tie the 7th thread. Holding these 4 threads together in LH, and using your RH, make a DDHH to the left with the 9th thread. Don't tie the 8th thread. Holding these 4 threads together in LH, and using your RH, make a DDHH to the left with the 10th thread. Don't tie the 9th thread. Holding these 4 threads together in RH, and using your LH, make a DDHH to the right with the 1st thread on the LS, as shown in the photo.

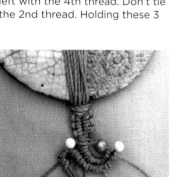 

8 Holding these 5 threads together in RH, and using your LH, make a DDHH to the right with the 2nd thread. Holding these 6 threads together in RH, and using your LH, make a DDHH to the right with the 3rd thread.

9 Holding these 6 threads together in RH, and using your LH, make a DDHH to the right with the 4th thread. Don't tie the 3rd thread.

 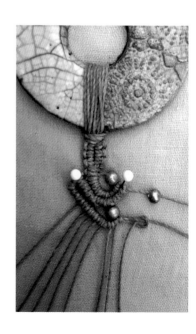

10 Thread beads onto the threads as shown in the photo. Holding 5 threads in RH, and using your LH, make a DDHH to the right with 1 thread. Holding 4 threads in RH, and using your LH, make a DDHH to the right with 1 thread. Holding 3 threads together in RH, and using your LH, make a DDHH to the right with 1 thread. Holding 2 threads together in RH, and using your LH, make a DDHH to the right with 1 thread. Holding 2 threads together in RH, and using your LH, make a DDHH to the right with the thread holding the bead.

11 Holding 1 thread in RH, and using your LH, make a DDHH to the right with 1 thread.

12 Holding the 1st thread from the RS in LH, and using your RH, make a DDHH to the left with all the threads.

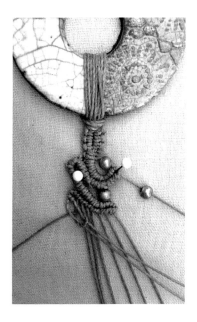

13 Holding the first thread from the LS in RH, and using your LH, make a DDHH to the right with the 2nd thread. Holding these 2 threads together in RH, and using your LH, make a DDHH to the right with the 3rd thread. Holding these 3 threads together in RH, and using your LH, make a DDHH to the right with the 4th thread. Holding these 3 threads together in RH, and using your LH, make a DDHH to the right with the 5th thread. Don't tie the 4th thread. Holding these 4 threads together in RH, and using your LH, make a DDHH to the right with the 6th thread.

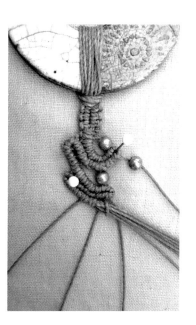

14 Holding these 5 threads together in RH, and using your LH, make a DDHH to the right with the 7th thread. Holding these 6 threads together in RH, and using your LH, make a DDHH to the right with the 8th thread.

15 Thread a round bead onto the 1st thread on the LS. Holding these 6 threads in RH, and using your LH, make a DDHH to the right with the 9th thread. Don't tie the 8th thread.

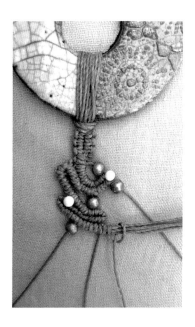

16 Holding 5 threads in RH, and using your LH, make a DDHH to the right with 1 thread. Holding 4 threads in RH, and using your LH, make a DDHH to the right with 1 thread. Holding 3 threads in RH, and using your LH, make a DDHH to the right with 1 thread. Holding 2 threads in RH, and using your LH, make a DDHH to the right with 1 thread. Holding 1 thread in RH, and using your LH, make a DDHH to the right with 1 thread. Continuing to hold the same thread using your RH, and using your LH, make a DDHH to the right with the thread holding the bead.

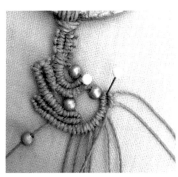

17 Holding the 1st thread from RS in your LH, and using your RH, make a DDHH to the left with all the threads.

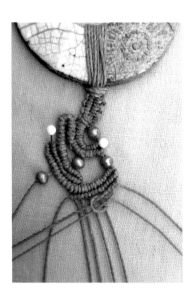

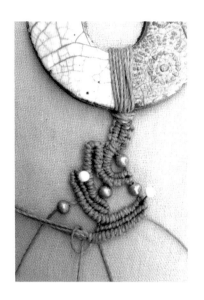

18 Holding the 1st thread from RS in LH, and using your RH, make a DDHH to the left with the 2nd thread. Continuing to hold the 1st thread in LH, and using your RH, make a DDHH to the left with the 3rd thread. Don't tie the 2nd thread. Holding these 2 threads in LH, and using your RH, make a DDHH to the left with the 4th thread. Holding these 3 threads in LH, and using your RH, make a DDHH to

the left with the 5th thread. Holding 4 threads in LH, and using your RH, make a DDHH to the left with the 6th thread. Holding 5 threads in LH, and using your RH, make a DDHH to the left with the 7th thread. Holding 6 threads in LH, and using your RH, make a DDHH to the left with the 8th thread. Holding 7 threads in LH, and using your RH, make a DDHH to the left with the 9th thread.

19 Continuing to hold 6 threads in LH, and using your RH, make a DDHH to the left with 1 thread.

20 Continuing to hold 5 threads together in LH, and using your RH, make a DDHH to the left with 1 thread. Repeat using 4 threads in LH, then 3, 2, and 1 thread. Holding the final thread in LH, and using your RH, make a DDHH to the left with the thread holding the bead.

Completing the Necklace

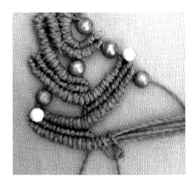

21 Thread a bead onto the 1st thread on RS. Holding 1st thread on the left in your RH, and using your LH, make a DDHH to the right with all the threads.

22 Holding 1st thread on the left in your RH, and using your LH, make a DDHH to the right with the 2nd thread. Holding these 2 threads in RH, and using your LH, make a DDHH to the right with the 3rd thread. Holding these 3 threads in RH, and using your LH, make a DDHH to the right with the 4th thread. Holding these 4 threads in RH, and using your LH,

make a DDHH to the right with the 5th thread. Holding these 5 threads in RH, and using your LH, make a DDHH to the right with the 6th thread. Holding these 6 threads in RH, and using your LH, make a DDHH to the right with the 7th thread. Holding these 7 threads in RH, and using your LH, make a DDHH to the right with the 8th thread. Holding these 8 threads in RH, and using LH, make a DDHH to the right with the 9th thread.

23 Holding 7 threads in RH, and using your LH, make a DDHH to the right with 1 thread. Holding 6 threads in RH, make a DDHH to the right with 1 thread. Holding 5 threads in RH, make a DDHH to the right with 1 thread. Holding 4 threads in RH, and using your LH, make a DDHH to the right with 1 thread. Holding 3 threads in RH, and using your LH, make a DDHH to the right with 1 thread. Holding 2 threads in RH, and using your LH, make a DDHH to the right with 1 thread. Holding 1 thread in RH, and using your LH, make a DDHH to the right with 1 thread.

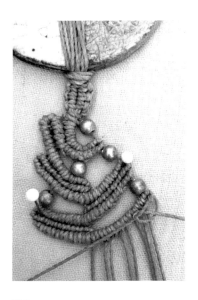

24 Continuing to hold the same thread in your RH, and using your LH, make a DDHH to the left with the thread holding the bead.

25 Using your LH, take the 1st thread from RS and, using your RH, make a DDHH to the left with all the threads.

26 Holding the 1st thread from RS in your LH, and using your RH, make a DDHH to the left with 8 threads. Repeat using 8 threads again, then 7, 6, 5, 4, 3, 2, and 1 thread. Holding the 1st thread from LS in your RH, and using your LH, make a DDHH to the right with 1 thread.

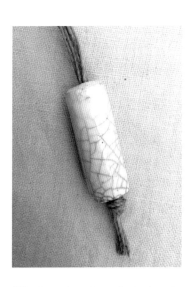

27 Holding 2 threads in your RH, and using your LH, make a DDHH to the right with 1 thread. Repeat holding 3, 4, 5, 6, 7, 8, and 9 threads in your RH.

28 Tie a large knot using all the threads 6⅝ in. (17cm) from the end of the work, thread a raku cylinder bead onto the threads, and secure it with a large knot.

29 Thread a raku cylinder bead onto the end of the threads and secure it with a large knot.

Fringed Necklace

A long fringe makes an eye-catching center-piece to this necklace. The fringe is embellished with a row of beads.

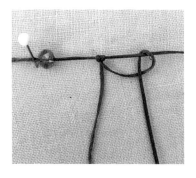

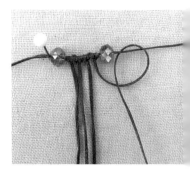

You Will Need:

One 35½ in. (90cm) length of 1/32 in. (1mm) gray waxed thread

Twenty 11⅞ in. (30cm) lengths of 1/32 in. (1mm) gray waxed thread

Two 23⅝ in. (60 cm) lengths of 1/32 in. (1mm) gray waxed thread

One 11⅞ in. (30cm) length of 1/32 in. (1mm) gray waxed thread

Nine faceted round beads, 3/16 in. (5mm) in diameter

Types of Knot:

HDHH: Horizontal double half hitch

RLH + HHEC: Reverse lark's head plus half hitch each cord

RLH: Reverse lark's head

SK: Square knot

Abbreviations:

LH: Left hand

LS: Left-hand side

RH: Right hand

RS: Right-hand side

Difficulty Rating:

Easy

Size:

Knotted section 5⅞ in. (15cm) long, length of necklace is adjustable

1 Lay the 35½ in. (90cm) length of thread horizontally, thread 1 bead, then add a 23⅝ in. (60 cm) length thread in the center using a RLH + HHEC.

2 Add a 23⅝ in. (60cm) length of thread in the center using a RLH + HHEC. Thread on 1 bead. With your LH, make a HDHH to the right with the 4th thread from the left, around the horizontal thread next to the bead.

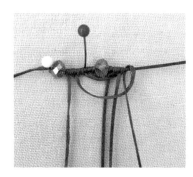

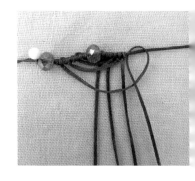

3 With your LH, make a HDHH to the right with the 3rd thread from the left, around the horizontal thread. Repeat using the 2nd thread to the right.

4 With your LH, make a HDHH to the right with the 1st thread to the right, around the horizontal thread.

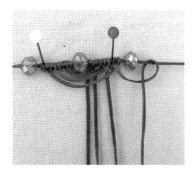

5 Repeat step 2 (from the point where you threaded 1 bead) to step 4 four times.

6 Thread a bead onto each end of the horizontal threads and knot the ends to secure them.

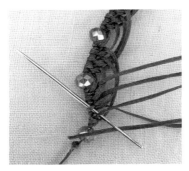

7 Using a RLH, attach four or five 1⅞ in. (30cm) threads to the bottom loop in each set of loops.

8 Thread a bead onto the RS of the necklace and tie a knot to secure it. Secure the ends of the threads on the back, trim, and seal them (see page 9).

9 With the horizontal thread pinned straight, trim the fringe so it is all the same length. Make a sliding closure (see page 12) using the final 1⅞ in. (30cm) thread and 5 SK. Secure the ends on the back as before.

Earth Tones Choker

The center of this choker is a simple, geometric design framed by bars of diagonal double half hitch knots and set off by coordinating beads. You can adapt the design to make a pair of earrings (see page 110).

(see page 110).

You Will Need:

Eight 67 in. (170cm) lengths of $^1/_{32}$ in. (1mm) brown Linhasita waxed thread

One 19$^5/_8$ in. (50cm) length of $^1/_{32}$ in. (1mm) brown Linhasita waxed thread

One 21$^5/_8$ in. (55cm) length of $^1/_{32}$ in. (1mm) brown Linhasita waxed thread

Four $^5/_{16}$ in. (8mm) brown round beads

Four $^1/_4$ in. (6 mm) brown round beads

Types of Knot:

DHH: Double half hitch

DDHH: Diagonal double half hitch

RDHH: Reverse double half hitch

RLH: Reverse lark's head

SK: Square knot

Abbreviations:

LH: Left hand

LS: Left-hand side

RH: Right hand

RS: Right-hand side

Difficulty Rating:

Advanced

Size:

Knotted section 10 $^5/_8$ in. (27cm) long, length of choker is adjustable

Starting the Choker

1 Take one 67 in. (170cm) length of thread and lay it horizontally. Attach seven 67 in. (170cm) threads in the center using a RLH.

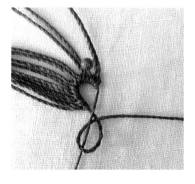

2 Hold 1 end of the horizontal thread with your LH, and use it to make a DHH with the other end of the thread to make a loop holding the 6 threads.

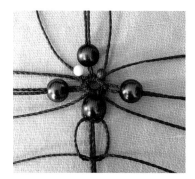

3 Divide the threads into 4 groups of 4 threads each. Thread a large bead onto the 2 central threads of each group, then make a SK with the 4 threads to secure the beads.

4 With the 2 left threads of each group, make 3 RDHH. Repeat using the 2 threads on the right of each group, reversing shaping.

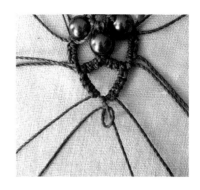

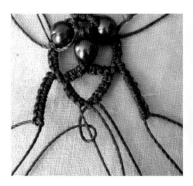

5 With the 2 threads on the LS that are vertical to the work, make 3 RDHH. Repeat using the 2 threads on the RS, reversing shaping. Hold the 2nd thread on the LS in your RH, and with your LH make a DHH using the 3rd thread.

6 Make 4 RDHH with the 2 central left threads and 4 RDHH with the 2 central right threads. Join the 2 central threads with a DHH.

7 Make 8 RDHH with the 2 external threads on both sides. Starting from the left, and with your RH, bring the 1st thread from the left (of the 4 central threads) to the right, and with your LH take the 2nd thread and make a DDHH.

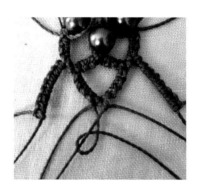

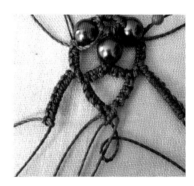

8 With your LH, take the 1st thread from the right; and with your RH, take the 2nd one and make a DDHH to the left.

9 With your LH, take the 3rd thread from the left; and with your RH, using the 2nd thread from the left, make a DDHH to the left.

10 With your LH, take the 1st thread on the right and bring it to the left. With your RH, take the 2nd thread and make a DDHH.

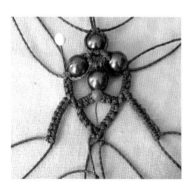

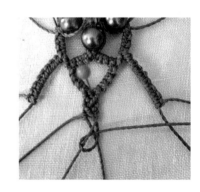

11 With your RH, take the 1st thread on the left and bring it to the right. With your LH, make a DDHH with the 2nd and 3rd threads.

12 With your RH, take the 1st thread on the left and bring it to the right. With your LH, make a DDHH with the 2nd thread.

13 With your LH, take the 1st thread on the right and bring it to the left. With your RH, make a DDHH knot with the 2nd and 3rd threads.

Completing the Choker

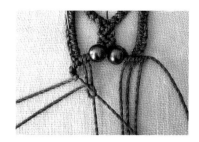

14 Thread a small bead onto the central thread on both sides. Starting from the left, with your LH, take the thread with the bead and make DDHH with the 3rd, 2nd, and 1st threads with your RH. Repeat with the threads on the RS, reversing shaping.

15 With your RH, take the 1st thread on the left and make DDHH to the right, using the 3 threads. Repeat using the 4 threads on the right, reversing shaping.

16 Repeat step 15 twice more. At the end of the 3rd bar of DDHH, cross the 2 central threads, making a DHH. Make another bar of DDHH on the right and the left and cross the central threads to make a DHH.

17 Repeat step 15 again from the right to the left and with a bar of DDHH using 3 threads, reversing shaping. Make a bar of DHH from the left to the right using 4 threads.

18 Make a bar of DHH from the left to the right using 3 threads.

19 Make a bar of DHH from the right to the left using 4 threads. Repeat steps 16 to 19 until you have 29 bars. Sew all threads except the 2 central ones to the back of the work to secure them. Trim and seal the ends (see page 9). Repeat steps 4 to 19 to make the other side of the choker, making sure you have the same number of bars and reversing shaping.

20 If the final combined length of the 2 central threads is not 9⅞ in. (25cm), add a new 19⅝ in. (50cm) thread (see page 9). Trim the threads so they are the same length. Make a sliding closure using the 21⅝ in. (55cm) long thread and 5 SK (see page 12). Finish the 2 threads on the back of the work (see page 9).

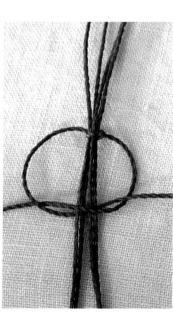

Variation

Earth Tones Earrings

You can adapt the design for the center of the choker (see pages 106–109) to make a pair of matching earrings.

You Will Need:

Sixteen 27½ in. (70cm) lengths of 1/32 in. (1mm) brown Linhasita waxed thread

Eight brown round beads, 5/16 in. (8mm) diameter

Two copper earwires

Types of Knot:

DDHH: Diagonal double half hitch

RDHH: Reverse double half hitch

RLHH: Reverse lark's head

SK: Square knot

Abbreviations:

LH: Left hand

LS: Left-hand side

RH: Right hand

RS: Right-hand side

Difficulty Rating:

Advanced

Size:

3⅛ in. (8cm) long

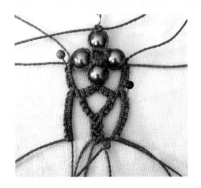

1 For each earring, follow the steps for making the choker to the end of step 13. With your LH, take the 2nd thread on the right and make a DDHH knot with the 3rd and 4th threads.

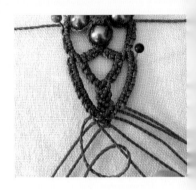

2 With your RH, take the 2nd thread on the left and make a DDHH with the 3rd and 4th threads. With your RH, take the 1st thread on the left and make a DDHH with the 2nd, 3rd, and 4th threads.

3 With your LH, take the 1st thread on the right and make a DDHH with the 2nd and 3rd threads. Join the 2 central threads with a DHH.

4 Sew all the threads to the back of the work to secure them. Trim and seal the ends (see page 9).

5 Use chain nose pliers to thread a copper earwire onto one end of the earring. Repeat to make a second earring.

Blue Beaded Necklace

Rows of double half hitch knots interspersed with blue and crystal beads create a long, elegant necklace with a bead fastening. The length is adjustable, so you can make it as long or as short as you like.

You Will Need:

Six 59 in. (150cm) lengths of $\frac{1}{32}$ in. (1mm) blue Linhasita waxed thread

One 63 in. (160cm) length of $\frac{1}{32}$ in. (1mm) blue Linhasita waxed thread

Four round jade beads $\frac{13}{32}$ in. (10mm) in diameter

73 faceted round crystals $\frac{3}{16}$ in. (5mm) in diameter

Types of Knot:

DDHH: Diagonal double half hitch

HKS: Half knot spiral

RLH: Reverse lark's head

SK: Square knot

VDHH: Vertical double half hitch

Abbreviations:

LH: Left hand

LS: Left-hand side

RH: Right hand

RS: Right-hand side

Difficulty Rating:

Medium

Size:

Knotted section 11 in. (28cm) long, length of bracelet is adjustable

Starting the Necklace

1 Position the 63 in. (160cm) thread vertically. In the center, thread a crystal, a blue bead, and a second crystal. At the same point, join a 59 in. (150cm) thread with a SK; a 2nd 59 in. (150cm) thread on the right; and a 3rd on the left with a RLH.

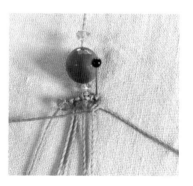

2 Thread a crystal on the 1st and the 3rd threads from the LS. With your LH, take the 1st thread on the right to the left, and use to make DDHH with all 6 threads.

3 With your LH, take the 1st thread on the RS toward the left to make VDHH with all 6 threads. With your LH, take the 1st thread on the right to the left, and use to make DDHH with all 6 threads. Repeat this series of knots.

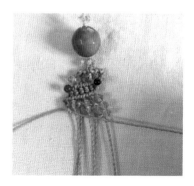

4 Thread 3 crystals onto the 1st thread on the right, 2 crystals on the 3rd thread on the right,o and 1 crystal on the 5th thread on the right. With your RH, take the 1st thread on the left to the right, and use to make DDHH with all 6 threads.

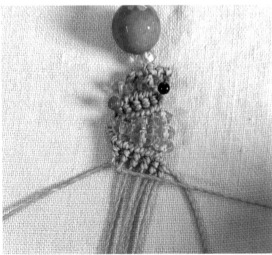

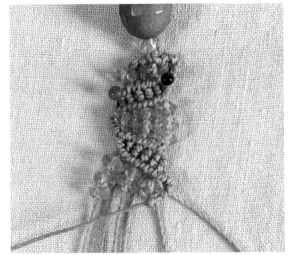

5 With your RH, take the 1st thread on the left to the right, and use to make VDHH with all 6 threads. With your RH, take the 1st thread on the left to the right, and use to make DDHH with all 6 threads

6 Thread 3 crystals onto the 1st thread on the left, 2 crystals onto the 3rd thread on the left, and 1 crystal onto the 5th thread on the left. With your LH, take the 1st thread on the right to the left, and use to make DDHH with all 6 threads.

Completing the Necklace

7 With your LH, take the 1st thread on the right to the left, and use to make VDHH with all 6 threads. With your LH, take the 1st thread on the right to the left, and use to make DDHH with all 6 threads. Repeat 6 times more.

8 Thread 4 crystals on the 1st thread on the right, 3 crystals on the 2nd thread on the right, 2 on the 3rd and 4th threads on the right, and 1 on the 5th and 6th threads on the right. Use the 2 side threads to make a HKS around the other threads.

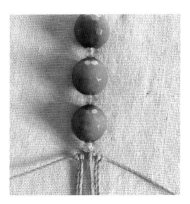

9 Continue to make HKS for 6⅞ in. (17 cm), threading a crystal every 1⅛ in. (3 cm). If you want a longer necklace, make more HKS here.

10 Thread the blue bead and make 3 more HKS. Thread a crystal onto the ends of the remaining threads and secure each one with a knot.

11 To work the 2nd side of the necklace, thread a blue bead, a crystal, a blue bead, and a crystal onto the vertical thread. Join a 59 in. (150cm) thread to the vertical thread with a SK, and the threads on the right and left with a RLH. Repeat steps 2 to 9.

Making the Loop Closure

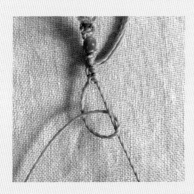

12 On one of the remaining threads, work 9 RDHH. With a needle, close the loop by sewing the threads to the back of the work so that the blue stone at the other end can pass through the loop. If it will not do this, increase the number of RDHH.

13 Trim and seal the ends of the threads (see page 9).

Agate and Raku Necklace

Rows of horizontal double half hitch knots frame the raku and agate beads that form the focal point of this pendant necklace.

You Will Need:

One 39⅜ in. (100 cm) length of ¹⁄₃₂ in. (1mm) Linhasita blue waxed thread

Fourteen 21⅝ in. (55cm) lengths of ¹⁄₃₂ in. (1mm) Linhasita blue waxed thread

One 47¼ in. (120 cm) length of ¹⁄₃₂ in. (1mm) Linhasita blue waxed thread

One 11⅞ in. (30cm) length of 1mm Linhasita blue waxed thread

Four ¹⁄₁₆ in. (2mm) gold beads

One raku cylinder bead 1³⁄₁₆ in. (3cm) long

Two agate beads, ¹³⁄₃₂ in. (10mm) in diameter

Types of Knot:

AEDHH: Accumulated edge using double half hitches

HDHH: Horizontal double half hitch

RLH + HHEC: Reverse lark's head plus half hitch each cord

SK: Square knot

Abbreviations:

LH: Left hand

LS: Left-hand side

RH: Right hand

RS: RS

Difficulty Rating:

Easy

Size:

Knotted section 2⅜ in. (6cm), length of necklace is adjustable

Making the Necklace

1 Thread an agate bead and then a gold bead onto the 39⅜ in. (100 cm) thread. Pass one end of the thread back through the agate bead and then both ends through the raku cylinder bead. The gold bead will secure the threads inside the other beads.

2 Add seven 21⅝ in. (55cm) threads with RLH + HHEC on the threads on both sides. Thread the ends of the 47¼ in. (120 cm) thread through the raku bead so that the ends extend from the base.

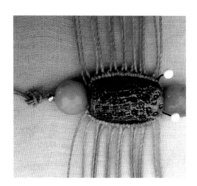

3 Thread the ends of the thread through the second agate bead and then a gold bead, and knot to secure.

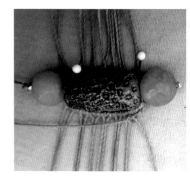

4 Using your LH, take the 1st thread from the RS and, using your RH, make a HDHH toward the left with all the threads.

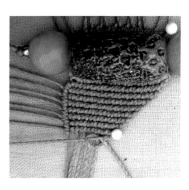

7 Using your LH, take the 1st thread from the RS and, using your RH, make a HDHH toward the left with the 2nd thread. Holding these 2 threads together in RH, make a HDHH toward the left with the 3rd thread.

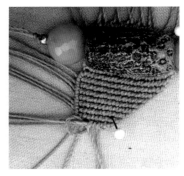

8 Holding the 3 threads in your LH, make a HDHH toward LS with 4th thread. Repeat with 5th and 6th threads but do not tie 4th and 5th threads. Sew threads to back of work, trim, and seal (see page 9). Repeat steps 4 to 8 on other side, reversing shaping.

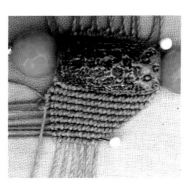

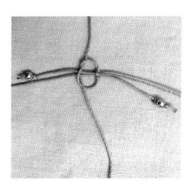

5 Using your LH, take the 1st thread from the RS and, using your RH, make a HDHH toward the left with 12 threads. Repeat using 11 threads, then 10 threads, and continue until you have made a HDHH toward the left with 6 threads.

6 Using your RH, take the 1st thread from the LS and, using your LH, make a HDHH toward the right with 7 threads.

9 Make a sliding closure (see page 12) using an 11⅞ in. (30cm) thread and 4 SK. Secure the ends on the back, trim, and seal them as before. Thread a gold-colored bead onto the ends of both threads and knot to secure them.

Raku Button Bracelet

A square raku-glazed pottery button is used to join two loops of thread knotted with horizontal double half hitch knots. You can replace the raku button with a glass or metal one if you prefer.

You Will Need:

Ten 31½ in. (80cm) lengths of ⅟₃₂ in. (1mm) gray waxed thread

One 11⅞ in. (30cm.) length of ⅟₃₂ in. (1mm) gray waxed thread

Seven ⁵⁄₁₆ x ³⁄₁₆ in. (8 x 5mm) hematite olive-shaped beads

One ¾ x ¾ in. (2 x 2cm) square raku ceramic button

Types of Knot:

AHH: Alternative half hitch

HDHH: Horizontal double half hitch

RLH: Reverse lark's head

SK: Square knot

Abbreviations:

LH: Left hand

LS: Left-hand side

RH: Right hand

RS: Right-hand side

Difficulty Rating:

Easy

Size:

Knotted section 4¾ in. (12cm) long, length of bracelet is adjustable

Starting the Bracelet

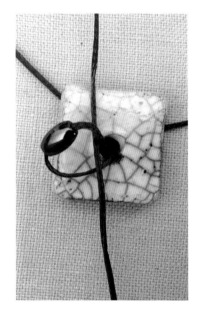

1 Thread the end of a 31½ in. (80cm) thread through the hole in the button, then add a bead and pass the thread back through the hole, so that it comes out at the back of the button. Thread another 31½ in. (80cm) thread through the thread holding the bead. Pull the two threads through to the back of the button.

2 Tie the top and bottom threads together on both sides of the button with an AHH.

3 Add a 31½ in. (80cm) thread with a RLH on both sides of the button.

4 Using your LH, take the 1st thread from the RS and, using your RH, make a HDHH to the left with 5 threads.

5 Using your RH, take the 1st thread from the LS and, using your LH, make a HDHH to the right with 2 threads.

6 Thread 1 bead and make a HDHH to the right with the last 2 threads.

7 Using your LH, take the 1st thread from the RH and, using your RH, make a HDHH to the left with 2 threads. Add a 31½ in. (80cm) thread with a RLH, make a HDHH with 1 thread (the one not knotted in step 6). Add a 31½ in. (80cm) thread with a RLH and make a HDHH with 2 threads.

8 Using your RH, take the 1st thread from the LS and, using your LH, make a HDHH to the right with 9 threads.

9 Using your LH, take the 1st thread from the RS and, using your RH, make a HDHH to the left with 4 threads. Thread 1 bead, don't tie the 5th thread, and continue to make a HDHH to the right with the last 4 threads.

10 Using your RH, take the 1st thread from the LS and, using your LH, make a HDHH to the right with 4 threads, then stretch the thread to the next 4 threads and continue to make a HDHH to the right with these 4 threads.

11 Using your LH, take the 1st thread from the RS and, using your RH, make a HDHH to the left with 4 threads.

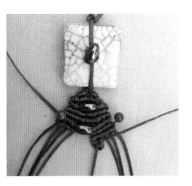

12 Working with the group of threads on the RS only, using your RH, take the 1st of the 5 threads from the LS and, using your LH, make a HDHH to the right with 4 threads. Repeat steps 11 and 12 until you have 9 bars.

13 Using your LH, take the thread not knotted in step 9 and, using your RH, make a HDHH to the left with 4 threads. Repeat steps 11 and 12 until you have 9 bars.

14 Put aside the 1st thread on the RS and the 1st thread on the LS (they will be finished on the back). Using your LH, take the 1st thread from the RS and, using your RH, make a HDHH to the left with 3 threads.

Completing the Bracelet

15 Using your LH, take the 1st thread from the RS and, using your RH, make a HDHH to the left with 3 threads. Repeat 2 more times. Repeat steps 14 and 15 on the LS, reversing shaping. Using your RH, take the 1st thread from the LS and, using your LH, make a HDHH to the right with 3 threads. Thread 1 bead and continue to make a HDHH to the right with 4 threads.

16 Put aside the 1st and 2nd threads on the RS (they will be finished on the back). Using your RH, take the 1st thread from the LS and, using your LH, make a HDHH to the right with 2 threads. Repeat on the RS, reversing shaping.

17 Make 2 SK with the 4 central threads.

18 Finish all the threads on the back (see page 9). Make the other side of the bracelet in the same way.

19 Make a sliding closure (see page 12) using the 11¾ in. (30cm) thread and 5 SK.

Naturally Beautiful Necklace

The beautiful grain and rich color of a piece of sanded and waxed wood makes it the perfect centerpiece for a necklace. Deep brown waxed thread and antique brass-plated beads make ideal partners.

You Will Need:

Seven 27½ in. (70cm) lengths of ¹/₃₂ in. (1mm) brown waxed thread

Two antique brass-plated oval buttons, ⁹/₁₆ x ¹³/₃₂ in. (15 x 10 mm)

Twenty-four brass-plated beads each with two small thread holes

Piece of smooth wood with channel around edge 2⅜ x 6 in. (6 x 15cm)

Types of Knot:

AEDHH: Accumulated edge using double half hitches

DHH: Double half hitch

HDHH: Horizontal double half hitch

HH: Half hitch

RLH: Reverse lark's head

Abbreviations:

LH: Left hand

LS: Left-hand side

RH: Right hand

RS: Right-hand side

Difficulty Rating:

Medium

Size:

Knotted section 3⅛ in. (8cm) long, length of necklace is adjustable

1 Position a length of thread around the channel in the wood. Add 4 threads with a RLH so that they sit at a narrow end. With LH, take the first thread on the LS to the left to make a DHH using your RH with the vertical thread.

2 With your RH, take the 1st thread on the LS to the right to make a HDHH using your LH with all 9 threads.

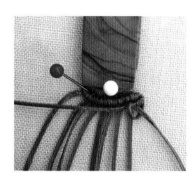

3 With your LH, take the 1st thread on the RS to the left to make a HDHH using your RH with all 9 threads. Repeat 7 times. Take the 5th central thread and the last thread on the right to the back.

4 With your LH, take the 4th thread from the LS and make a HDHH to the left using your RH and the 3rd thread. With these 2 threads in your LH, make a HDHH to the left using the 2nd thread and your RH.

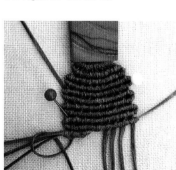

5 Keeping the 3 threads just worked in your LH, make HDHH to the left using your RH with the 1st thread.

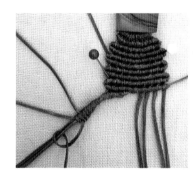

6 Add 1 thread with a RLH. With your LH, hold the 5 threads together and, using your RH, make 6 HH to the left. Use a thread from the group to make 1 HH. Repeat 4 times, but do not use the longest thread.

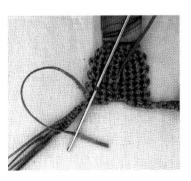

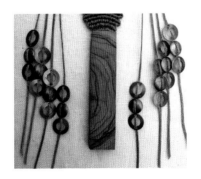

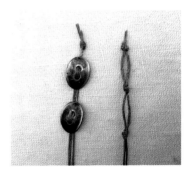

7 With your RH, take the 4th thread from the RS and make 1 HDHH to the right using your LH with the 3rd thread. Repeat steps 4 to 7. Sew the 2 threads at the back of the work; trim and seal (see page 9).

8 Thread 3 beads on each thread, as shown in the picture or as you prefer. Knot and cut the threads holding the beads.

9 To secure the necklace, thread the buttons at one end of the long threads, and with two knots create the buttonholes in the other end as shown in the photo.

Chunky Raku Bracelet

The textured surface of this square raku bead
is complemented by a network of different half
hitch knots to create this eye-catching bracelet.

You Will Need:

Fourteen 47¼ in. (120cm)
lengths of ¹⁄₃₂ in. (1mm) black
waxed thread

One 11⅞ in. (30cm) length of
¹⁄₃₂ in. (1mm) black waxed thread

1 raku ceramic square bead
with grooved sides, 1³⁄₁₆ x 1³⁄₁₆ in.
(3 x 3cm)

Types of Knot:

AEDHH: Accumulated edge using
double half hitches

AHH: Alternative half hitch

DDHH: Diagonal double half hitch

HDHH: Horizontal double
half hitch

RLH + HHEC: Reverse lark's head
plus half hitch each cord

SK: Square knot

Abbreviations:

LH: Left hand

LS: Left-hand side

RH: Right hand

RS: Right-hand side

Difficulty Rating:

Medium

Size:

Knotted section 7⅞ in. (20cm)
long, length of bracelet is
adjustable

Starting the Bracelet

Tip

If the thread around the raku bead is not tight enough, you can
secure it with a dab of clear glue.

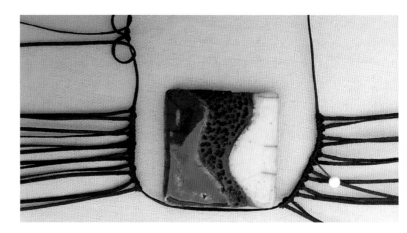

1 Place a 47¼ in. (120cm) thread
against one side of the raku
bead. Using a RLH + HHEC, add
seven 47¼ in. (120cm) threads to
the left and six 47¼ in. (120cm)
threads to the right, as shown in
the photo.

2 On the RS (with 6 threads),
join 2 threads with a DDHH as
shown in the photo and fasten
them as tightly as you can
around the raku square.

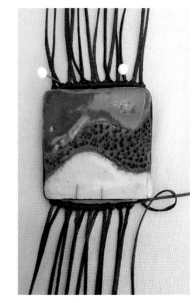

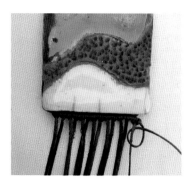

3 Make 6 AHH with the 1st and 2nd threads on the RS.

4 Make 5 AHH with the 3rd and 4th threads; 4 AHH with the 5th and 6th threads; 3 AHH with the 7th and 8th threads; 2 AHH with the 9th and 10th threads; and 1 AHH with the 11th and 12th threads, as shown in the photo. Using your RH, take the 1st thread from the LS and make a DDHH toward the right with the 2nd thread.

In the Know

You can make the bracelet smaller by working fewer alternative half hitch chain knots.

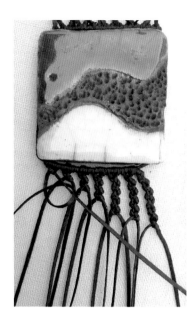

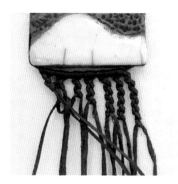

5 Holding these 2 threads together in your RH, make a HDHH toward the right with the 3rd thread.

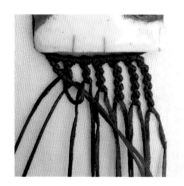

6 Continuing to hold these two threads together in your RH, make a HDHH toward the right with the 11 remaining threads.

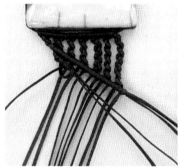

7 Using your RH, take the 1st thread from the LS and make a DDHH toward the right with the 2nd thread. Holding these 2 threads together in your RH, make a HDHH toward the right with the 3rd thread. Continue with the 9 remaining threads.

8 Repeat step 7 with 10, 8, 6, 4, and 2 threads.

9 Make 6 AHH with the 1st and 2nd threads on the RS. Make 6 AHH with the 3rd and 4th threads, 6 AHH with the 5th and 6th threads, 6 AHH with the 7th

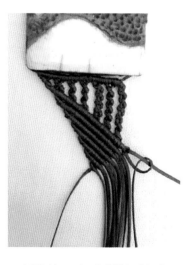

and 8th threads, 6 AHH with the 9th and 10th threads, and 7 AHH with the 11th and 12th threads.

10 Using your RH, take the 1st thread from the LS and make a DDHH toward the right with thread 2. Using your RH, take the same thread and make a DDHH toward the right with the 1st and 2nd threads from the RS.

Completing the Bracelet

11 Using your RH, take the same thread and make a DDHH toward the right with the 3rd and 4th threads from the RS. Repeat until the 11th and 12th threads from the RS have been used.

12 Make 11 AHH with the 1st and 2nd threads from the LS.

13 Make 8 AHH with the 3rd and 4th threads, 7 with the 5th and 6th threads, 5 with the 7th and 8th threads, 3 with the 9th and 10th threads, and 2 with the

11th and 12th threads. Using your LH, take the 1st thread from RS and make a DDHH toward the left with the 2nd thread. Holding these 2 threads together in your LH, make a HDHH toward the left with the 3rd thread. Continue with the 11 remaining threads.

14 Using your LH, take the 1st thread from the RS and make a DDHH toward the left with the 2nd thread. Holding these two threads together in your LH, make a HDHH toward the left with the 3rd thread. Continue with the 9 remaining threads.

15 Repeat step 14 with 10, 8, 6, 4, and 2 threads.

16 Using your RH, take the 1st thread from the LS and make a DDHH toward the right with the 2nd thread. Holding these 2 threads together in your RH, make a HDHH toward the right with the 3rd thread.

17 Holding these 3 threads together in your RH, make a HDHH toward the right with the 5th thread. Continuing to hold the 3 threads together in your RH, make a HDHH toward the right with the 7th, 9th, 11th, and 13th threads.

18 Finish 11 threads at the back of the work (see page 9). The three remaining threads must be the ones which will be used for the sliding closure. Repeat steps 3 to 18 on the other side of the bracelet, reversing shaping.

19 Make a sliding closure (see page 12) using the 11⅞ in. (30cm) thread and 5 SK. Secure the ends on the back, trim, and seal them (see page 9).

Star Pendant Necklace

A series of star-shaped beads are joined by rows of half hitch knots to create a dramatic pendant centerpiece for this necklace.

You Will Need:

Nine 59 in. (150cm) lengths of $\frac{1}{32}$ in. (1mm) deep blue-green waxed thread

One 11 $\frac{7}{8}$ in. (30cm) length of $\frac{1}{32}$ in. (1mm) deep blue-green waxed thread

Twenty $\frac{5}{16}$ in. (8mm) hematite star beads

Six $\frac{9}{16}$ in. (15mm) star beads with two holes

Types of Knot:

DDHH: Diagonal double half hitch

HDHH: Horizontal double half hitch

RLH: Reverse lark's head

RLH + HHEC: Reverse lark's head plus half hitch each cord

SK: Square knot

SKB: Square knot button

Abbreviations:

LH: Left hand

LS: Left-hand side

RH: Right hand

RS: Right-hand side

Difficulty Rating:

Easy

Size:

Knotted section 4$\frac{3}{4}$ in. (12cm) long, length of necklace is adjustable

Making the Necklace

1 Position a 59 in. (150cm) thread horizontally. Add another in the center with a RLH; make 10 SK. Make a SKB. Add 2 more threads on both sides with RLH + HHEC. Using your LH, take the 6th thread from LS and make DDHH toward the left with 5 threads.

2 Using LH, take 6th thread from LS and make DDHH toward left with 5 threads. Repeat 4 times. Repeat on RS 6 times. Thread a large and small star onto 6th thread from LS. Using RH, take 1st thread on LS and make DDHH toward right with 5 threads.

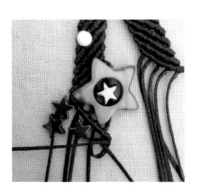

3 Thread 2 small stars onto the 1st thread on LS and 1 onto the 3rd thread. Using your LH, take the 6th thread from the LS and make HDHH toward the left with 5 threads.

4 Using your RH, take the 1st thread from the LS and make HDHH toward the right with 5 threads. Repeat 8 more times.

7 Using your RH, take the 1st thread from the RS and make DDHH toward the right with 5 threads. Repeat 6 more times.

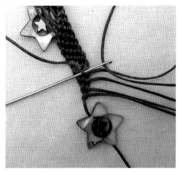

8 Thread a large and a small star onto the 6th thread from the LS. Finish 5 threads at back of work (see page 9). Repeat steps 3 to 8 on the RS.

5 Thread 2 small stars onto the 1st thread from the LS and 1 onto the 3rd thread. Using your LH, take the 6th thread from the LS and make HDHH toward the left with 5 threads.

6 Thread a large and a small star onto the 6th thread from the LS. Using your RH, take the 1st thread from the LS and make DDHH toward the right with 5 threads.

9 Make a DDHH with 2 threads. Thread a small star onto the ends and knot. Make a braid 35½ in. (90cm) long using the remaining 59 in. (150cm) threads. Make a sliding closure (see page 12) using the 11⅞ in. (30cm) thread and 5 SK. Secure the ends.

Star Pendant Necklace **127**

Index

Acknowledgments

I would like to thank Publisher Ellen Dupont and Editor Julie Brooke who have accompanied me during the months I spent writing this book, gave me the willpower and the right support I needed, and were always kind and patient. Working with them has allowed me to grow and improve my knowledge.

Also many thanks to Francesco Piccolo (ritrattifotografici.com) for his beautiful photography and Linhasita threads (exportacao@linhasita.com.br) and RAKULAB ceramics (info@rakulab.it, www.etsy.com/it/shop/RAKULAB) for their help with materials.

Photo p.7: 123RF Magdalena Kucova

Morena Pirri
@morenamacrame
www.etsy.com/it/shop/morenamacrame
https://morenapirri.wordpress.com/